THE BABY ROOM

Dr Amanda Norman

THE BABY ROOM

A Person-Centered Approach to Communities of Practice and Belonging Within Formal Day Care

The Education Studies Collection

Collection Editor

Dr Janise Hurtig

This book is dedicated to Xavier, Pandora, Cassius, and Lola who have nurtured and supported my journey.

First published in 2024 by Lived Places Publishing

All rights reserved. No part of this publication may be reproduced, stored in a retrieval system, or transmitted in any form or by any means, electronic, mechanical, photocopying, recording or otherwise, without prior permission in writing from the publisher.

The authors and editors have made every effort to ensure the accuracy of information contained in this publication, but assumes no responsibility for any errors, inaccuracies, inconsistencies, and omissions. Likewise, every effort has been made to contact copyright holders. If any copyright material has been reproduced unwittingly and without permission, the Publisher will gladly receive information enabling them to rectify any error or omission in subsequent editions.

Copyright © 2024 Amanda Norman

British Library Cataloguing in Publication Data
A CIP record for this book is available from the British Library

ISBN: 9781915734860 (pbk)
ISBN: 9781915734884 (ePDF)
ISBN: 9781915734877 (ePUB)

The right of Amanda Norman to be identified as the Author of this work has been asserted by them in accordance with the Copyright, Design and Patents Act 1988.

Cover design by Fiachra McCarthy
Book design by Rachel Trolove of Twin Trail Design
Typeset by Newgen Publishing UK

Lived Places Publishing
Long Island
New York 11789

www.livedplacespublishing.com

Abstract

This book contributes to a timely connection between the understanding and application of a Person-Centered Approach (PCA) within formal day care. Developed by Carl Rogers, PCA will be discussed in relation to the value of how an understanding about a humanistic psychological perspective can be useful when caring for infants in formal day care.

The book is intended to be read by those interested in working with infants, as part of a team within a PCA approach. It includes the principles of a therapeutic relationship and how these could be applied within care and educational contexts, as well as chapters dedicated to the role of supervision. It therefore aims to be a useful book resource—with informed practices included as well as case study examples provided —regarding the complexities and appreciation of working with infants. Focus will be on how the social identity of the professional is shaped when working in the baby room and how a sense of belonging can be achieved. These are included from an auto-ethnographical methodology to illustrate the author's perspective as a professional in ethically supporting infants, as well as colleagues in their experiences.

Keywords

Person-Centered Approach; Baby room; Practitioner; Key person; Infant; Early education; Play; Belonging; Supervision; Teamwork; Listening; Empathy; Congruent; Community; Parent relationship

An author's message

The book is intended to be an informative guide about connection, understanding, and both being part of the community and developing a sense of community. The book aims to be the catalyst in developing a sense of belonging within early years contexts and strengthening the network of working with infants in baby rooms.

This book aims to develop understanding about working in a baby room in formal day care. It highlights the lived experiences of the complexities around ethical care when working with infants under two years of age. It also reflects on the social identities of the practitioners working as a community of practice and the challenges around maternal discourse and professional care. It offers a person-centered framework in developing a sense of belonging and community.

Author's background

Dr Amanda Norman is a Senior Lecturer of Childhood Studies at the University of Winchester, UK. She is the author of *From Conception to Two: Development, Policy and Practice* (2019) and has published works about infant care pedagogies in academic peer reviewed and professional practice articles. She is also the sole author of the book *Historical Perspectives on Infant Care and Development*, with Bloomsbury Publishing. Amanda is currently researching spiritual and infant care relationships, from historical and contemporary perspectives. As a practicing therapeutic play specialist and early years consultant, she continues to support and liaise with early professionals working in the sector, in addition to her academic role.

Language

In choosing the terms for the book, I have considered what I think to be the most appropriate and contemporary phrases, often found in the literature or when communicating with groups as well as within policy documents. I have also aligned terms such as the baby room and key person that are familiar to those working in the UK.

Contents

An author's message		vi
Author's background		vii
Language		viii
Introduction		1
Chapter 1	A Person-Centered Approach to communities of practice and belonging in formal day care	13
	Learning Objective: Communities and belonging	14
Chapter 2	A community of infants: Working in the baby room in formal day care in England	35
	Learning Objective: Baby room practices and the practitioner's role	36
Chapter 3	A personal approach to a PCA of working ethically with infants	65
	Learning Objective: Complexities of baby room communities	65
Chapter 4	A community of practice: PCA supervision in the baby room	85
	Learning Objective: Valuing supervision as a listening approach	85

| **Chapter 5** | A community of practice: Teamworking in the baby room | **111** |

Learning Objective: Working together as a team to support well being and good mental health for both themselves and the infants in their care **111**

Conclusion	**131**
Recommended discussion topics	**139**
References	**142**
Recommended further readings	**149**
Index	**151**

Introduction

This book explores the lived experiences of working in the baby room of a formal day care setting and how a Person-Centered Approach (PCA) could be helpful in developing deeper reflections about belonging, interactions with others, and promoting a community of practice. Developed by Carl Rogers, a humanistic psychologist working within professional counselling, a PCA recognizes the value of being empathic, listening to others, and being honest and authentic within relationships. The book explores the practices within formal day care when working with young children. It specifically explores personal experiences and practices of working with birth to two-year-old's in the baby room. I have used the term "formal day care" within each chapter, and this includes early years centers, nurseries, family centers, childminders, and any other service offering early years care and education for infants and toddlers. The baby room I discuss are the spaces inhabited by those working with infants in formal day care. I have also referred to "infants" rather than "babies and toddlers" and assume that infants encompass birth to two years of age, unless specified otherwise.

This book includes anecdotal and shared experiences from my previous role of managing a day nursery and leading practice in the baby room, as well as reflections from thirty years' experience of working with children, their families, and professionals within and beyond the local community. The book also includes other practitioners' stories and vignettes, including their emotional and ethical demands of working with infants, an area worthy of further research. Some of these stories are parts of situations or combined narratives to highlight some of the practices I want to share. I have therefore purposefully anonymized case studies to ensure that what I chose to share is ethical and doesn't compromise those I know.

The thread of the book includes the principles of how a PCA shapes therapeutic relationships and how these could be applied by professionals working with infants as well as each other. It therefore aims to be a useful book resource, with informed practices included and lots of illustrations to highlight the complexities and appreciation of working in a baby room.

Practitioners in early years contexts have a dual task of caring for infants and caring for themselves as individuals. When caring for infants from birth, we all recognize it as being a precious, vulnerable, and fast-changing transitional stage of life. Emotions, communication, and physical development are arguably the most prominent areas to understand and engage with during this age, and the relationships between practitioner and infant can be challenging and complex as well as joyful and rewarding.

I only really appreciated the complexities of the relationship when I had been in practice for a few years and once I began to reflect with a critical eye, becoming more honest and open about my experiences with caring for infants, without fear of judgment. Prior to this I had been restricted to pockets of theory, observations of infants, and colleagues' practices. I was also relying heavily on my own subjective experiences, childhood, and cultural context upbringing. While I considered my own perspective as positive and validating my pedagogical thinking, it remained a narrow lens in approaching experiences and events with the infants I cared for. Once I began to understand the theory and processes of reflection, I then begin to explore and wrestle with my limitations, prejudices, experiences, and forward thinking.

Reflecting on practice has been taught within early years courses for several years, particularly with professional enquiry-based learning courses (Moon, 2013). Today, many areas of employment with children now require a reflective approach within their work cycle, through regular reviews or appraisals. Typically, this means taking personal responsibility for:

- Continuing professional development;
- Evaluating personal experience, strengths, qualities, and skills as part of a role;
- Identifying ways that personal strengths can be used within a professional area;
- Identifying training, practice, or informal learning in supporting personal limitations and areas that could be improved; and
- A way of taking responsibility for behavior and making useful contributions.

From a PCA, the purpose of reflection should, therefore:

- Be a way of theorizing on our actions;
- Develop confidence;
- Develop an active agent in the daily routine of care;
- Support an agency of change;
- Increase recognition and knowledge that empowers and improves quality;
- Enable our vulnerability to be discussed and shared with colleagues;
- Challenge and develop our own pedagogical thinking; and
- Advocate for children in activity evaluating multiple perspectives and development.

Reflective practice of practitioners is an increasingly familiar term when working in a caring profession, especially when it is an expected approach to practice and linked to quality improvement. As early years practitioners, we are continually thinking about creating exciting learning experiences for the infants we work with. As a practitioner, when outside of the work setting, how many times have you stopped yourself discarding some household box, crockery, or a basket with the consideration that it could be used for some kind of play activity? This type of thinking beyond our time at work becomes habitual and automatic in our everyday lives. This 'way of being' forms an aspect of our professional identity. Through questioning our actions to why we think about our practice within and beyond our work setting, enables a professional creativity and inspiration to be developed, as described by Schon (1983; 1987).

In thinking about this further, we begin to see reflections as shaping our thinking and behavior. Reflective activism is about having a critical consciousness of the world whereby we question, examine, and challenge different positions including our own actions and thoughts; this involves 'active engagement in continual review and repositioning of assumptions, values, and practice' (Hanson, 2012, p. 144, in Trodd, 2015). We reflect about our upbringing, how we are parented, and how this influences our own practices as childcare professionals. It involves thinking about the wider sociocultural landscape and how it influences the current context practitioners work in. In being a reflective activist, it also enables us to consider how theory directly informs practice as a bridge to creating new meanings and consequently exploring different possibilities and solutions. This could be related to many aspects of care from the way we support infant sleep to how we engage and think about play with them.

Stephen Brookfield (1995) provided a way of critically reflecting in teaching, which continues to be relevant in early years contexts when caring for infants. Four lenses of critical reflection are applied as a way of illuminating different aspects to teaching and one that can also be applied to early years practice, mirroring the lenses to this text in terms of infant development, theory, and practice. I have used Brookfield's lens in my previous work, *From Conception to Two Years* (Norman, 2019), and in articulating how I view the importance of refection. It is an appropriate model to consider and, below, I illustrate the way practice and reflection come together, and why I think they are valuable in application to critical reflection.

Infant (student) lens

To organize the environment, practices, and support the infant's development, we need to try to find out what is going on within the infant and gain their perspectives on the care and education they experience. The student lens in early years is therefore about trying to understand how the infant learns and feels in given situations. For Brookfield, it is recognizing that those remarks and actions we as practitioners think of as insignificant, are interpreted quite differently by the infant (student) when played back. In working with infants, I recognized this in thinking about the ethics of care and how we use not just our verbal communication but also our expressions and gestures in supporting the infant in learning and developing successfully. How we project our own feelings and actions in the baby room, such as laughing or being unresponsive, can be interpreted by the infant as a significant signal to how they are feeling valued. It is therefore the lens that considers the power relationship and the power of the role that is given. If we assume, as I propose, that infants are creative, autonomous agents, then they have the capacity to be critical of their care—either responding verbally or physically in signaling that they want to be noticed, cuddled, talked to, and handled in a certain way. While many practitioners state they welcome criticism from the children in their care in differing forms, there are few that will honestly receive it positively and, in the case of the infant, regardless of the activities, the environment, or behavior, the fault for them not fully reaching their potential is generally considered to be in the infant rather than the practitioner's actions (Norman, 2019). The lens of the infant's reveals how your practice is viewed from differing perspectives and reinforces how differing approaches should be, not just with, for example, play activities but how those play activities are approached by individual infants. I think, in working with the youngest infants, it is also about reflecting on the power position and how we work ethically. By recognizing our authority in the relationship and what we project in supporting infants throughout the day, potentially provides the capacity to reflect and interact together in everyday routines, such as nappy changing, feeding, and sleep times, rather than reverting to an instructional approach. It is the balance between leading and caring (Brooker, 2010).

Co-practitioners (colleagues) lens

In some ways, this encompasses positive teamwork and how, as work colleagues, we can support each other. This lens is about becoming critical friends with work colleagues and sharing advice. Wenger's (1998) concepts of building communities of practice is about creating an open and honest space to share troubles and successes and, for him, it is therefore about listening and not just agreeing and praising each other but also being honest and expressing stresses and anxieties, too. Sharing insights into a given situation enables colleagues to appreciate that dilemmas are not unique and, by offering multiple perspectives and viewpoints, cannot just help in solving problems but assist in re-examining them in differing ways.

Autobiographical (personal) lens

In early years this is a valuable reflective lens in listening to the voices of practitioners working in early childhood education and care. For those working with infants, the stories told can often hold more value and insight to the theory surrounding them. It is the personal telling of a story that can be identified with and, in some cases, shape and justify the work of practitioners. In many ways, our own pedagogies are embroiled into how we practice. Our own personal experiences of learning, our own values and upbringing all play a significant role in how we deliver practice in the present context. How we view our own childhood and school experience with authority figures also impacts how we react. Another aspect to the relationship between infant, parent(s), and practitioner is the emotional engagement and investment of caring for infants. Being paid to care can be challenging because it is about the emotional labor of the work and therefore includes tensions surrounding how much investment is necessary and how it is different to parent relationships.

For myself, I remember spending time with an infant who needed constant reassurance that her mother was returning to get her. The infant was about 14-months-old and they were aware of a change in their care and surroundings. In a bid to support them, I had to make decisions not just with their care but the others I was also caring for, so they did not become frightened and upset by the sporadic and frightened crying. I had to decide if the lunchtime transition should be changed to accommodate the infant since they would not eat, in the initial phase. I needed to consider if I should have a lunch break, knowing the separation would be really challenging for them. I had to reassure colleagues that, together, we could support each other although, at the time, the infant would not leave my side and I had additional responsibilities to carry out as part of my job. I wanted to be there to receive the infant at 8 a.m. and then feedback to the parent at 6 p.m. in order to develop a triad relationship rather than trying to replace the parent role, even though I was only expected and paid to work seven hours a day.

While this was and continues to be a familiar scenario of settling infants by reflecting on the process, I began to critique my own position in the relationship and how I could move forward positively. I reflected on theory in framing my approach, but I was equally drawn to thinking of those subjective stories of past experiences that I recalled as a way of supporting the infant-practitioner relationship during the day. Remembering personal and shared experiences and events provides another lens as a way of how I perceive my role, how I embark on the relationship, the time frame I set myself, and available flexibility within a given day. The shared support with colleagues and the settling in procedures in supporting the infant and myself in developing a positive relationship, mirrors not just the ethos of the setting but also supports my own pedagogical thinking. This includes tensions and stressful situations to be resolved in harmony rather than the imposed upon strategies that can be alienating and abstract to the daily experiences that occur in some early years settings.

Theoretical lens

The final lens of critical refection is theory and, in theorizing the early years, there are numerous journals, books, and magazines to draw on. However, for many in practice, theory can often remain disconnected to what is experienced. Journal articles can have an academic tone and many practitioners would seldom go to them if they had a particular enquiry. However, theory is presented in many forms, not just within articles. In my own personal journey initially engaging with readings, I was drawn to Rogers (1980) and the way he discussed relationships in a person-centered way. At the time, I was working with vulnerable families and had been met with aggressive behavior. I was feeling, in part, vulnerable but mostly inadequate in why I thought I could help in the relationships, having concerns that I was expected to be a counsellor or provide solutions. It was through reading his work and applying some simple strategies that I could listen to parent's complex situations from an educational and caring perspective.

As I entered different roles, I went from a diagnostic way of thinking to observing and listening, moving forward, and valuing the art of listening. Person-centered thinking is about allowing the space for people to find themselves rather than telling them the way to go. As a leader, it sparked an approach that gave autonomy, recognizing the potential in others rather than imposing a model to conform to. By engaging in varied job roles with colleagues, parents, and infants, I have managed to apply Rogers' work to my relationships. In developing congruence, being true to myself, and accepting of my thoughts and feelings, I was able to share these authentically. In accepting others, I have been able to develop a positive regard and caring approach in the form of a non-possessive love. I have also been able to empathize within my work and strive to provide genuine understanding.

These three areas are what Rogers believes are essential to moving forward and, for me, the theoretical underpinning of the approach was relatable. Subsequently this led me to develop my thinking about humanistic psychology and the subjective self. I developed my practice within a Froebelian philosophy, which places play central to learning, regarding the inner capacity of the infant and the value of the adult relationships. My work was skewed again when I embarked on a play therapy course. While

I was confident in my work as a practitioner of young children, I had not appreciated how I was portrayed by the children in the relationship. By refocusing on myself within a therapeutic relationship, I found the theoretical frame critiques and modified how I approached children in their play. I learned to listen and slow down, metaphorically and literally, following the guiding principles of a PCA (Norman, 2019). An example of this is during feeding times with an infant and being aware of their needs and observing their responses. I spoke to the parents about their home feeding routine and how this aligns with what I do in the day care setting. When I feed an infant, I record how much is consumed and their preferences, if they are being weaned. I reflect on the way I have created a calm and nurturing time for the infant and feed with care. Critical reflection is therefore evident when contemplating a theoretical lens. It enables both the opportunity to reflect on theory itself and what resonates with one's own pedagogy alongside how theory is approached in relation to contemporary practice.

In outlining a PCA and Froebelian principles of ensuring the child is at the heart of care, by starting where the child is rather than where I think they ought to be I hope this provides a taster to a broad range of themes included in this book. It aims to navigate the reader toward specialist subjects and concepts. Care and tuned in relationships are key to early childhood education, and yet therapeutic approaches to support emotions are often left to external experts or those undertaking specific training in addition to their early years qualifications. The book also explores how educators can be supportive through empathy, understanding, and congruence in developing relationships.

1
A Person-Centered Approach to communities of practice and belonging in formal day care

Key points for consideration from the chapter:

- Human psychology focuses on the individual and the capacity for growth;
- A PCA is an opportunity to think about how we engage with individuals in our everyday life, both within and beyond work;
- How we view infants and their capabilities, and how we interact with them as professionals;
- How our own life story influences our professional practices; and
- Why a PCA is a worthy contribution for practitioners working in the baby room.

Learning objectives

To think about and reflect on setting communities and belonging when working with infants.

To begin to understand a Person-Centered Approach and how this could be adopted when working with infants.

A Person-Centered Approach (PCA) is viewed as a set of values, skills, and tools that can be useful in getting to know someone, what they find important, and what they want out of life. Beyond counselling, where person-centered therapy historically resides, a PCA can be thought of as a philosophy, a way of thinking, or a mindset which involves viewing, listening to, and supporting a person or child, based on their strengths, abilities, aspirations, and preferences regarding the decisions to developing and maintaining meaning in their life. A Person-Centered Approach and thinking are therefore considered the basis for action in all kinds of situations, from planning to organization, and understanding and connecting with communities.

My journey to developing and practicing a PCA

At the start of my career, I trained in what was known as a 'nursery nurse' qualification. It was a new vocational course, being an alternative but an equivalent to completing subject courses that allowed entry into university if I wished to do so. I remember having a turbulent school time, having moved and finished formal schooling at 15 years of age. I was not considered academic, and I think the expectation was for me to meet someone and begin a family. I was determined to be able to complete the nursery nurse course, and I think this determination came from wanting to be a teacher and knowing that I would like to work in education, preferably with young children. I had gained work experience, so I was familiar with what to expect, although the irony hadn't been missed in me wanting to work in school education after desperately trying to escape it for almost five years.

The course was true to its word and in studying, doing vocational placements, and writing about children, I immersed myself in all the subjects and felt I belonged to a group, a profession, and connected with my present and future. I was no longer in the 'outgroup' as Kelly (2005) evaluated in his studies. I was now part of a larger network that placed children at the center of their work. This experience has not really left me, and although I was considered a hard worker but perhaps not one for university, I continued to carve out a career for myself, nervously following unknown paths and territories with curiosity and concerns. I did go to university and, from then, have viewed myself as a lifelong learner and an advocate for children.

Several years later, I became a co-owner and manager of a formal day care setting, leading in the pre-school and then baby room. Within the early years sector, there continues to be a move towards working with the older children, with an emphasis on their learning and interests. I too was motivated to do this and trained in teaching older children. However, I began to recognize that the infants, those between the ages of birth to two years, were needing more support and I was often popping into the baby room and reassuring the parents on their care as well as supporting the other practitioners. We then had a change of staff, and it was at this point that I decided, as manager, to become the baby room lead and support the infants and staff in there. Initially it was to be for about six months until we recruited someone, but, in the end, I spent many years in the baby room. Even with breaks in other areas, I would return and work part-time in the baby room. The experiences I gained from working with infants and practitioners is one of the main motivations for developing research and further training. I learned about the complexities of infant care; from what type of food the infants were fed to their individualized sleep patterns. I also grew confident in being able to support and soothe the infants and worked closely with the other staff in the baby room as well as the parents. I do not think enough is spoken about reading the daily lived experiences of being in the baby room and how a sense of belonging is necessary for the room to be successful. I have since worked with many practitioners also in the baby room, and they often share their experiences, mirroring my own.

A central area I wanted to explore when I worked in the baby room was how we form common ground in our practices: the way we interact and approach a caring and compassionate pedagogy. During the time I spent in the baby room, I had responsibility for infants from birth (generally it was from six weeks of age) to two years, some attending up to 50 hours a day. How do I retain a non-judgmental approach? What do I do when the parents insist on certain practices that contradict what we are doing in the baby room? How do I support the practitioners to make sense of the policies we follow but also work ethically and with a love of their vocation? How do I manage and lead both staff and children when a high turnover of staff one summer creates shifts in the dynamics of the group? I have attempt to

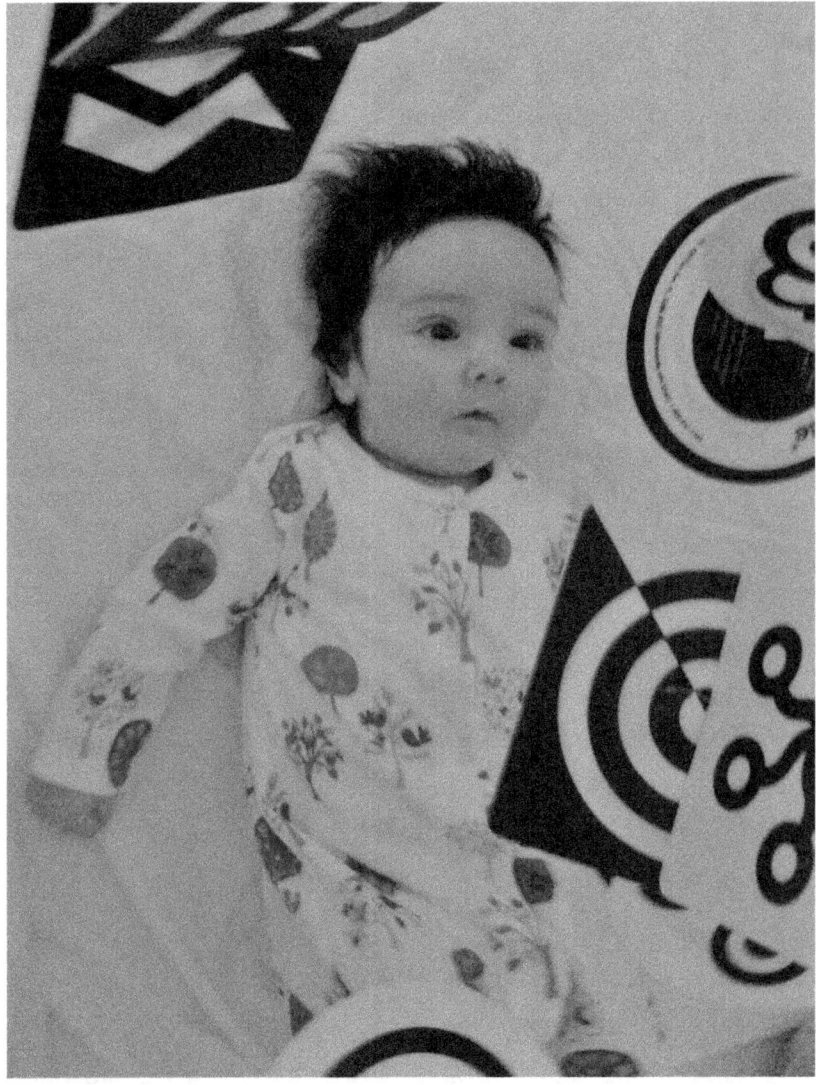

Figure 1 Innovative play ideas for infants when working with parents.

answer many of these questions and more in this book but, initially, I want to journey towards the Person-Centered Approach and why I consider this to be a valuable approach to working in the baby room.

As I noted earlier, I continued training and completing professional development courses from the degrees I studied. For my master's in education, I focused on children with special needs and counselling. It was the counselling that shined a light on how I could work in alternative ways! I was familiar with the behaviorist approach of focusing on children's behavior and strategies to promote positive behavior. I was less familiar with working as a team of practitioners, caring for infants as well as working with what I considered, at times, stressed and demanding parents, often relying on what I had observed through practice and picked up along the way. I think at times I had a 'them and us' approach when working with the parents. On the one hand, I had an expert position as a trained individual, but I was also deeply anxious and insecure about whether my position was a cover for a feeling of imposter syndrome. During this time, I had not had any children, so I was not able to draw on my experiences as a parent either. I do not feel this is an essential element when working with children, but it certainly brings another dimension to my understanding about parents' experiences. In relation to team working, I would navigate towards those team members who were less confrontational and would be quite authoritative, although I would avoid challenging conversations. As a result, I often ended up doing more than my share in the allocation of jobs.

By having a work break and studying counselling, I was able to consider how people think, feel, and behave, and how this can all be related to or completely disconnected from their way of being. I learned that individuals move into parent, adult, and child mode dependent on the context and who they are talking to (Bernes, 1958). I also learned about how to respond to an adult who is unresponsive, angry, apathetic, or just rude. There was no crystal ball, but there were techniques and ways I could listen and meet them halfway, with empathy and listening without judgment. Although I was not training as a counsellor, I was learning the counselling approaches and principles offered in the different modalities of counselling. This resonated with me. Having worked for a couple of years with families with young children whose parents were deemed high risk and in vulnerable situations, from homelessness to drug use, I began to apply these principles in my work. I was able to talk to the parents about the care of their children authentically and compassionately. They were often angry and scared of their situation, and I was often shouted at or aggressively spoken to. By applying these principles, I could retain some control of the potential conflict and diffuse the atmosphere without feeling and looking overwhelmed. For example, I remember a parent shouting at me because they had received a letter about attending a parenting group assuming I had initiated the plan even though I had not been involved in the decision-making.

Another confrontational incident that occurred was when an infant had got paint on their dress and the parents were cross, concerned the paint would not wash out. During both incidents I remained calm and suggested ways of moving forward. I nodded and ensured the parents were heard. I acknowledged their anger but spoke in a calm manner. I repeated what they said to ensure I understood what was bothering them and, through a PCA, was able to share an action plan and diffuse the situation.

From this experience, I moved into professional training as a therapeutic play specialist where I focused on working primarily with children therapeutically. I was exposed to how the sand tray could be a mode of communication, the objects as symbols; art, dance, and creative activities could not only have a learning emphasis but also a therapeutic emphasis. I initially found the work quite challenging and unfamiliar to the everyday approaches I had used when working with children. I had to learn to slow down and, essentially, not speak! The aim was to listen and avoid filling the silences with learning opportunities. I did note that I was more controlling than I thought I would be, and it opened my eyes to self-refection in a much more meaningful way.

Integrating counselling approaches into formal day care settings

One of the concerns of educators and myself was encouraging those who were not a specialist in counselling or play therapy to think they can practice and diagnose children and their needs. There are of course specialists with specific training in play therapy to support children's individual needs. In working with children every day in care and educational contexts, a therapeutic approach is not about being a therapist but considering how the principles could be included in a practitioner's everyday experiences of working in the baby room (with both the infants and the practitioners), in meeting their personal, emotional, and social needs. Judit Horvath (2021), a manager who also worked in a nursery, wrote that play is communication that can have considerable therapeutic benefits. As she highlights, the principles of play therapy can be aligned to everyday practice.

Virginia Axline (1974), also a renowned play therapist famous for her book *Dibs in Search of Self*, included a set of principles about how professionals could work in a person-centered way. This included how to approach relationships to:

- Develop a warm and friendly relationship with the child, and
- Accept the child as they are not what they should or could be.

Many of these areas are what would be expected if working as a play therapist or other type of role with children (Axline, 1974; Horvath, 2021).

A person-centered approach therefore includes a framework to reflect on emotional relationships, meeting emotional and social needs, space to communicate together, and work creatively together to support wellbeing (Horvath, 2021). For infants to thrive and have positive outcomes, they need unconditional acceptance to grow a healthy self-concept, and this can be achieved by supporting and co-regulating their feelings. Unconditional positive regard is at the heart of a PCA, accepting individuals for who they are without judgment. A focus for the practitioner, working with infants is therefore being a companion and facilitator. This works with the practitioners as a team too and, in creating conditions for self-development and personal growth, practitioners can move towards their true potential in a constructive way. In practice, I remember when two infants (who were under three-months-old) began attending. This caused some anxiety with the newer and less experienced practitioners. Together, we implemented some changes around rest time and feeding. We bought a rocking chair for the room for allocated feeding, so both the practitioner and infant would feel relaxed and comfortable together. We also ensured that a member of the team was free to care for the infant individually during the day, outside of feeding and changing. This was to develop a bond with the infants and encourage good attachments. The parents were also spoken to at the end of the day and follow up conversations were shared the following morning. While this was encouraged with all the infants in the baby room, we ensured a little more time was given to the allocated practitioner so they could speak to the parents without feeling rushed or concerned about doing something else in the room.

By developing a way of trying to understand the individual's inner world in co-regulation, it also promotes a genuine approach. In working with staff at a formal day care, I noted what the PCA could offer, reflecting on my own experiences and, by engaging in a PCA, it provided me with a theoretical understanding and practice to how communication, including listening, can be so powerful in daily interactions. PCA was a journey about working with colleagues, parents, and children.

CRIB: connecting principles with everyday practice
A Person-Centered Approach (PCA) to a CRIB of Care
Baby room relationships in formal day care

In developing a PCA, the model has been designed to aid practice (see CRIB of Care) as a visual way that could be included when working within a PCA. Each subsequent chapter will highlight an outlined element, but it all aims to place the **child at the heart** of the Person-Centered Approach (PCA). I have considered how care can be, both from a feeling's perspective as well as a thinking perspective, to enhancing relationships both working together with co-workers, infants, and their families,

My starting point is to think about what and how we emotionally engage in the baby room when we are working with infants and one other within the team.

I draw from an emotional perspective to think about how this would occur and the ways this could be achieved when moving towards a thinking perspective.

From an emotional perspective, **becoming** is the focus rather than fixed and this can be applied to personal and intimate relationships. An emotional lens also includes being personal and attuned relationships between infant and the practitioner. It can also include thinking about how we work ethically and the professional love we convey in the **intimate relationships** we create with the infants in our care.

In thinking about **compassionate care**, I think about the **respect**, empathy, and warmth towards the infant, having a valued understanding, and the importance of that in caring for them.

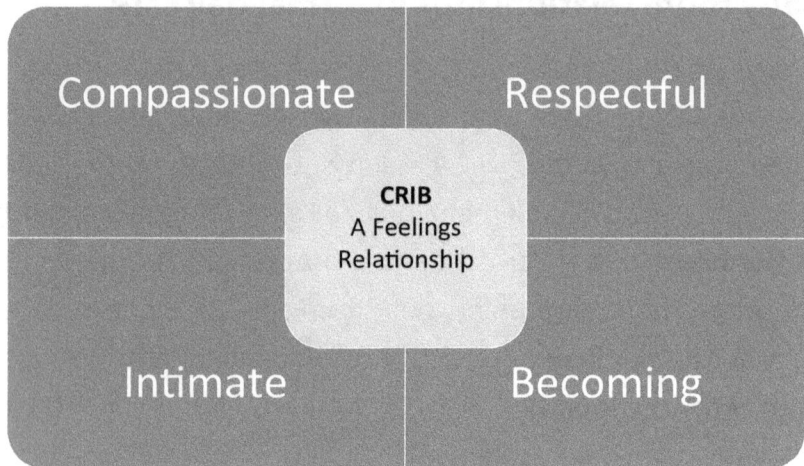

A Person-Centered Approach (PCA) to a CRIB of Care
Baby room relationships in formal day care

When I think about a thinking relationship, for me it is about being **curious** in my everyday work experiences. Being curious about the way I respond and feel with the infants I care for as as well as being curious about everyday practices and how relationships are nurtured.

A **rights**-based approach, for me, is about reflecting on the rights to play and creating opportunities for infants to be active agents. This can be challenging for nonverbal children, and it is about thinking of ways beyond speech that they can share their voice being in an autonomous learner thinking relationship. It is also about being **interactive,** creating reciprocal relationships with the infants in our care and listening to them through nonverbal communication.

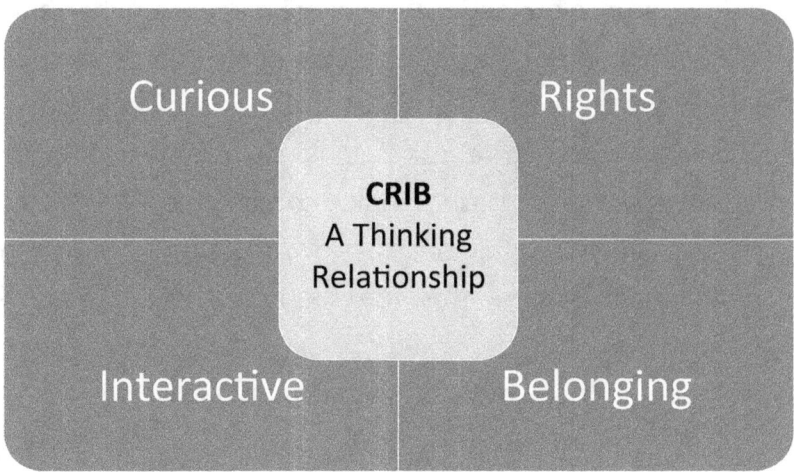

The history of a PCA

Humanistic psychology is often referred to as the "third force" in psychology. It is the way that each of us are intrinsically involved in the process of existence, being a distinct individual immersed in the flow of experience and moving through life. This approach agrees that, in most situations, we are aware of having some autonomy and a sense of empowerment with the ability to make choices. The power of choice in action allows the opportunity for us to decide who we would like to become. It is a process described as personal growth and humanist psychologies are there to support individuals through their desired change as they experience it. The focus relates to an understanding of feelings in themselves and exploring alternatives. Taking a holistic approach, the core of the experience is the flow of conscious awareness. One of the influential humanistic psychologists was Abraham Maslow (1962), who discussed how we reach this through our needs being met. He stated this was not often linear, although, once our physical needs are met, we are then able to be interested in our safety and secure needs, then a sense of belonging and self-worth. In moving towards the peak experience, it will have its own intrinsic meaning and wholeness to the person experiencing it. Maslow indicated that peak experiences ignited in a variety of situations (Maslow, 1962. These can often be from mundane experiences, from sitting with family and having a meal or walking home after having studied intensely for several hours, to those more significant moments in life such as giving birth (Maslow, 1962).

Maslow believed that peak experiences have the potential to stimulate individuals to reflect on their own experiences and the potential, available possibilities before them. The flow experience is personal and the complete involvement in an activity experience is enjoyed for its own sake. This is often a state I wonder if infants immerse themselves in much more readily in their experiences than we do as adults. A further assumption within humanistic psychology is that individuals are basically good and have an innate need to make themselves and the world better (Hoffman, 1994). For me, this is an outlook I would agree with in terms of the infants I care for and the practitioners I work with. Humanistic psychology therefore moves away from making generalizations about individuals and focuses much more on the personal worth of the individual. It is an optimistic perspective in the human capacity to overcome hardship, pain, and despair.

Carl Rogers was also widely recognized for this work in humanistic psychology (alongside Maslow) and, in Britain during the 1960s, he initially drew attention around marriage guidance counselling. Rogers' work was then increasingly disseminated and studied in British universities and within school counselling training courses. He defined a fully functioning person as being able to seek out new experiences physically and psychologically, as well as mastering new skills (Sanders, 2021).

For Rogers (1969), a fully functioning person could be open and to experience existential living, trust, be creative, and autonomous in their decision making. He also believed that, from childhood to adulthood, positive regard was believed to be key to personal growth; positive regard being the affection, approval, and acceptance needed from the important people in children's lives (particularly parents), unconditionally. Having positive self-regard influences and enhances self-esteem, self-worth, and positive self-image. This is enhanced through interactions which are:

- Congruent – based in genuineness, honesty with the client;
- Empathic – demonstrating the ability to feel what the client feels; and
- Respectful and understanding – showing acceptance, an unconditional positive regard towards the client (Corey, 1996, p. 202; Rogers, 1951).

In Rogers' application of PCA, he did not focus on problems and solutions but approached the person holistically in the relationship. For him it was about how two individuals (in his work, it was between the counsellor and client) can invest themselves freely and fully in the relationship, gaining entrance into the world of another. For him, the relationships are perceived as an emotional commitment. This is similar, in my view, to when we work daily with practitioners and with the infants in our care. As a leader, I do not assume I am all-knowing, distant from the practitioners I engage with because the goal is for them to become a fully functioning person with good psychological health, working together harmoniously. It is invested relationships, and the intention is towards valuing honesty and the capacity of accepting and evaluating oneself and one's own feelings. Respect and understanding of others and nurturing close relationships, with a willing to risk being open to all in everyday experiences and this in turn trickles down to respectfully caring for the infants we work with (Tolan, 2003; Sanders, 2021).

Working together in the baby room of a formal day care

Working together as a harmonious team is relevant to working in the baby room because if we can't work well together as a team, how can we support the infants we are caring for? I was fortunate to work with three to four other staff, and we would have a maximum of ten infants in our care at any one time, often having around eight. This was intentional in ensuring that we developed and maintained rich relationships and supported one another. While it could be argued this was a small number and therefore perhaps evoked intense relationships in the baby room, I wanted to create a sense of place and space, which takes time, thought, and reflection. However, in taking the time to reflect on teamworking, its aims to promote a sense of place builds and therefore having a feeling of belonging. In working with my team, we would often consider and reflect about:

- How was the place and space special and/or unique?
- How were these special qualities created?
- How could these be enhanced?
- What could we do to move ideas into objectives in the baby room we worked in?
- What routines and rituals do we share, and were these daily, weekly or monthly?
- How are positive attachments formed?
- How do we include parents to feel a sense of belonging?

I consider that maintaining a similar physical level encourages relational body language that offers good eye contact between the two, creating safe spaces and offering relationships that are respectful and meet the other individuals on their level, with sensitivity and sincerity (McCormack and McCance, 2016).

Unconditional positive regard is about reducing assumptions of judgments in creating positive and accepting attitudes. Change is more likely to occur when the practitioner is willing to be emotionally engaged with the individual, showing empathy, honesty, and unconditional positive regard. Empathic understanding is experienced and communicated. In accepting them for who they are, they in turn can become more nurturing as they feel really listened to and more attentive to their inner experiences (Rogers, 1980, p. 117).

A PCA is therefore not a repertoire of techniques, but rather an individual's system of underpinning values and an integrated aspect of that person's continual process. In thinking about this further, it is perhaps worth reflecting about engaging with individuals. Ask yourself:

- How authentic were you with the team members you work with?
- Do you provide unconditional positive regard when team members talk about something that is worrying them or happened to them, and they want to be listened to?
- Do you think you have empathic understanding?

In thinking about this more broadly, bridging a PCA with a sense of belonging is one of the areas I had previously engaged in, regarding what we all had to offer in the baby room. I would ask new practitioners if they had a particular interest or something they did in their own lives beyond work. This was always quite revealing and, in the past, I have worked with novice and professional saxophone players, pianists, dancers, artists, and clothes makers. I have also worked with footballers, bakers, and even Star Trek fans! All these other skills, interests, and areas of expertise can often be brought to life when working together and forming a community of practice and strengths-based approaches. In asking what the practitioners could share with the setting, they were able to draw on their strengths and assets, working together in harmony. An example of this was when a practitioner one day revealed that she could play the flute at an advanced level. She did not seem to appreciate the value of this and, after speaking to her, she was keen to develop a rest time involving music and develop recordings for parents to take home. This was a tremendous confidence boost for the practitioner, and she began to communicate more generally once she shared her experience of playing the flute.

Often when practitioners initially enter the baby room, they can feel intimidated since they may be lacking in experience. They may feel awkward coming into a new day care culture but, in building on their culture capital, we can really harness their strengths. Cultural capital is the practitioner's social assets and differences, such as education, knowledge, and experiences, that they can bring and contribute as part of the community they work in. Practitioners may also want to build on a skill as well or learn something new, and that can also be rewarding on both a professional and personal level. Sharing roles and distributing the leadership in the baby room offers an opportunity for everyone to lead rather than be led. This also ignites responsibility and motivation in working with the infants.

Psychologist Carl Rogers writes that clients often enter counselling in a state of incongruence; they are often confused about who they truly are and who they believe they must be to be accepted as a person (Rogers, 1980). For him, a PCA accepts that a client may have a desperate need for external authority and part of the work of the counsellor is to avoid falling into that trap by adopting the role as the authoritarian person, telling them what to do. Instead, the relationship is about walking alongside them on their journey of self-healing and self-growth.

I resonate with this in my own practice and feel this is something we can all do in our caring roles for infants and each other. We have the capability to provide the emotional holding space for infants, but acknowledge that all emotions, even uncomfortable ones, should be recognized, felt, and processed rather than avoided or suppressed. Rogers proposes that when we were young, we began to develop a self-concept, and if we think we are worthless or unacceptable, then we validate this through negative behavior so that chances of getting approval or esteem are further reduced. I have observed this in both adults and infants, and children I have professionally worked with, and agree it is about giving them space and increasing autonomy, as they need it, in supporting their own growth and development as an individual. For infants, a personal identity and the sense of who we are, according to Bowlby (2005), is closely dependent on the few internal attachment relationships we have or have had in our lives. Upbringing influenced by those close to us can be secure or insecure, loving or neglectful (Bowlby 1988). Therefore, close relationships are considered significant and influential to how a child makes sense of their world. As Carl Rogers highlighted, self-actualizing and being one with the self in adulthood comes from having relationships that emphasize the following:

- By being congruent with them;
- Providing unconditional positive regard; and
- Having an empathic understanding (Rogers, 1980).

This is not just concerned with attending to emotional needs but also creating opportunities for agency of voice, events with nonverbal infants, as illustrated by Gerber (2001). Gerber evaluated that adults, particularly in western cultures, have become too invested in doing everything to or for the infant rather than allowing them their own personal freedom in finding their own way (Gerber, 2001. She shared the desire to encourage practices that were supportive for infants and created opportunities for families to listen to the child, allowing them to be active. As an educationalist, I view person-centeredness within a PCA to be a relational and compassionate care pedagogy. It encourages the slowing and making of meaningful interactions within the fast-paced macro and micro societies in which both children and adults live. It could be considered, in part, a contemplative pedagogy, and the purpose of this chapter is for the reader to develop connections and meanings for themselves in understanding more about a PCA.

2
A community of infants

Working in the baby room in formal day care in England

Through communication and play, infants are often choosing how much they openly share with others. Within a relaxed, present, engaged, and non-judgmental caregiver more is shared, communicated, and known about each other and themselves. The therapeutic principles make common sense to those working in early years, offering environments that are welcoming, engaging, safe, secure, and open to all. This enables opportunities for open honesty and healthy attachments. Play is always a creative act whereby individuals develop narratives, imagine, and explore the world. In therapeutic play, the child is given the opportunity to explore without limitations or boundaries. For the child, it is about establishing a feeling of permission in the relationship so that the child can freely express themselves. Therefore, practitioners should consider the following in working with infants:

- Be alert to the feelings the child is expressing and reflect these feelings back in such a manner that the child gains insight into their behavior;

- Maintain a deep respect for the child's ability in finding solutions to problems as they occur, giving the child the time and opportunity to do so;
- Avoid attempting to direct the child's actions or conversations in any manner as the child leads the way;
- Avoid hurrying the time along as play is a gradual process, with many facets; and
- Only establish those limitations necessary to anchor the time to the world of reality and to make the child aware of their responsibility in the situation (Axline, 1974).

A case study exploration into a community of infants

This chapter is a personal journey as a senior leader working in the baby room. By sharing personal experiences, I hope it enables others to reflect on their practices and the complexities of working in the baby room. Focusing on play and communication, I have chosen to use anonymized case studies to illustrate the various ways of working with infants. Each case study is introduced and then the reflections of practice will be discussed. Reflections within a PCA are then shared regarding the significance of the case study in illustrating baby room practices.

Learning objective

To think about baby room practices and the practitioner's role of caring for babies, and how the PCA offers a valuable approach to working.

To consider a sense of belonging and how this can be achieved in the baby room.

My position in sharing the case studies.

Carroll (2013) argued that being reflective requires the individual to situate their personal, political, intellectual, theoretical, and autobiographical self during all stages of the research and interactional processes. Reflection is about a growing self-awareness, in relation to the environment in discussion and from the perspective of others. Through the process we must ask ourselves how our role is shaped by our personal experiences and how these are enmeshed in the world we find ourselves in and how the social contexts influence what we edit in and what we decide to omit. For me, this includes reflecting and drawing attention to how power influences attitudes and behaviors in my own role, shaping the experiences of myself as well as others. I acknowledge I was the leader in the baby room and, therefore, my perception (as they occurred) is personal to me and are from my own lens. The validity and reliability I draw upon is based on the conversations and the extent to which I worked in the baby room and how the experiences began to broadly mirror previous experiences. Of course, all the experiences, infants, and practitioners I engaged with were unique and individual but there were threads of practices, approaches, and understandings from wider reading that enabled some patterns to emerge and develop, with a deeper and more critical understanding about the infants I cared for.

Figure 2 Learning from the infants.

Case study 1
Introduction to the infant

Molly was four-months-old when she started attending the baby room and I was leading in. I hadn't been in the baby room long and, during this time, had gained some experience with infants, but not this young. Molly had a mother and a father and was living in the local area. She was living in a two-bedroom apartment and had her own room prepared but was currently still in her parents' bedroom, being breastfed as well as bottle fed. The language the parents spoke was English and Molly was their first child.

When a child begins, irrespective of age, we generally have a settling in period, which comprises of a few sessions with parents as well as the child on their own to become familiar with their surroundings. The sessions are all varied and can be individualized regarding the length of time, addressing what the parents are hoping to know and how the child's needs are being met during the settling in time.

During the settling in meeting, it was established that Molly's mother had been unwell and would be returning to work in the next few months. The childbirth had been traumatic and there were concerns that Molly may have cerebral palsy, but none of this information was given by the GP. The father would be bringing Molly in the mornings and collecting her in the evening. Molly would be attending the baby room full time between the hours of 8 a.m. and 6 p.m. She had been introduced to formula milk the previous month and would have the same brand at the setting, as well as offered breast milk from expressed milk or during nightly feeds. The feeding bottles given to Molly would also be the same. Within the settling in period, Molly was quiet and the dad held her close, wrapped in a blanket.

The mother was also present with the settling in time. The mother looked tired but appeared interested in what the nursery would be offering and how her daughter would be cared for. She seemed a little anxious that she wouldn't be the person dropping off or picking up, as this would primarily be the father. He was reassuring and seemed to understand this was challenging for the mother.

There felt a little resistance in the process but acceptance at the same time. I had to be mindful that I was not making judgments about the situation and, while I was concerned the infant was very young, it was my role to support the parents and the infant in our care. I understood the rationale for why they were doing this and felt empathy for the mother. I actively listened and reassured them. I did not rush to take Molly for a cuddle and allowed them to give her to me in a respectful way. I was also conscious of ensuring all the feeding and equipment necessary was documented.

Once Molly began attending the baby room, she seemed settled and was allocated to one person (myself) who would be leading on her care.

Reflections of practice
Diaper changing

Due to Molly being very young, she was supported in her communication and play, within and beyond everyday care routines. During her diaper changing time, I would take the opportunity to sing to her and talk to her while she was being changed. Molly would make eye contact with me and make gurgling noises. She had quite long limbs and would stretch them out when she was ready to be changed. I would also give her a cloth to play with while she was being changed, which she would take to her mouth and hold, grasping it tightly. Molly was generally quite vocal during changing time and was responsive to the way I talked to her. Sometimes, if she had soiled her diaper and I changed her, she would look away. This was a sign that she was a little bit uncomfortable. She would kick her legs up and move them about while she was being changed. I was very mindful that, during her first few months in the baby room, I was meeting her emotional needs but also her physical needs as these were changing quite rapidly within her development.

Feeding

Having had little prior experience with bottle feeding, I hadn't appreciated how many bottles were on the market as well as how many teats were on offer. Not only were the shapes and size of the bottles significant but the teats, with their various sized holes, indicated how much or little milk was offered to the infant during feeding. This was a learning curve for me. Understanding the types of feeding methods used for such a young infant, we communicated this in the settling in sessions and managed to get the same bottles and formula milk as she had at home. She was still being breastfed every evening, but the mixed feeding approach seemed to be working satisfactorily. I would make the feeds up and I would ensure that this was a quiet time. During feeding, I ensured she was spoken to and stroked gently.

Molly fed quite quickly but would never take all the milk that was suggested by the parents. They wanted to encourage her to have six to seven ounces and she was more inclined to have four to five ounces. I had to think about how I would ensure that she was getting enough to feed during the day because we had her for several hours each day. This was causing me some anxiety in terms of knowing that, if she lost weight, this would be a very big concern for her age. For any age it is a concern but at 12 weeks old, I wanted to ensure that she was getting the nutrients she was supposed to. I felt I was emotionally invested in her care and this labor of love was a mix of stress and warm regard.

Sometimes, during the day, this was quite challenging because there were some other infants in the room who were slightly older but also needed my attention. While I was trying to ensure

I gave her qualitative individual time, quite often other children would come along and want my attention. Simultaneously, I didn't want to feel rushed. However, during several occasions, I felt I was rushing unintentionally, and I don't think this helped the relationship. I think Molly noticed I was rushed and began stopping and starting with her milk feed. As she was being fed, I initially settled in a big rocking chair. It was helpful to create a calming ambience and one-on-one time. However, if there was less staff in the room, this was quite challenging because it meant that the other member of staff had to be responsible for my other two children that I was key person for. It then became easier to pop a cushion on the floor to be down on the children's level while I was feeding her, being able to have eye contact with the other infants as well as feeding Molly. This seemed to work better and, because I was on the floor, the other infants didn't seem to come and approach me as much as when I was sat on the higher chair, hanging and wobbling around it.

Molly fed as well with me on the floor, and it was interesting and something I hadn't foreseen before I think in terms of her character and thinking about feeding and diaper changing. During the weeks of caring for Molly, she was increasingly wanting my attention, listening to what I was saying, and we were tuning into each other during these intimate moments. She was also very receptive to how I responded to her and how I initiated conversations with her. She seemed quite calm at four-months-old, although sometimes it took a little longer to feed than anticipated. I therefore slightly shortened the time in between just to ensure that she was getting the right amount of milk. I also had to write down the amount of milk, monitor it regularly, and ensure this was correct and clear for the parents.

Reflective accounts within a Person-Centered Approach

Reflecting on a PCA involved thinking how I could be authentic in the everyday care moments of working in my role as practitioner. For very young infants like Molly, routine care such as diaper changing, feeding, and sleeping are very much part of the of a play experience as well as building caring connections. Often these routines almost take a procedural approach, and it would have been easy to quickly change her diaper with little engagement, getting the deed done, and moving on to the next infant for changing.

For me, it was important to include these care activities in almost the same way as play activities. I needed to think about what would be beneficial for Molly in terms of her experiences during these everyday routine times. Feeding was important, especially as she was being breastfed, so I had to be authentic and really listen to what she was trying to communicate to me as a non-verbal infant. I was also noticing when she was having a diaper changed and was a little bit sore, that I met her physical needs but also her emotional needs, by telling her what I was doing and asking permission to change her diaper. Of course, I knew that she couldn't say yes or no, but it was about respecting that interaction that I had with her. I felt I was implementing a PCA with her.

Case study 2
Introduction to the infant

Josh was 14-months-old and during his settling in time, when he came to visit the baby room, he was brought in by his mother. She had recently moved to the area and was living in rented accommodation in the next town. Josh's mother worked in retail and, although travelled occasionally, the shop she was based at was local to the setting. Josh would be full time, attending the ten hours a day we were open because his mother was the manager of the shop. His mother had a new partner and Josh's biological father was not present in their lives. Josh was of mixed heritage, and this seemed to concern his mum who was Scottish while Josh's dad was West African. She was concerned about how he would be responded to and referred to his heritage several times in conversation during the visit. She also decided that she didn't want to have his photo included in any of the publicity brochures.

She also talked about Josh's development from birth and felt, as he was getting older, he was becoming quite difficult to manage. Josh's mother stated she had tried to respond to him positively but was finding sleep time quite challenging. She had recently resorted to putting him in the buggy and positioning the seat flat to allow Josh to go to sleep, rather than using a bed.

Josh's mum shared that she had previously employed an au pair, but this had ended as they moved, and she wanted to provide Josh with some stability. This was the main reason she had decided to bring Josh to the nursery setting. Josh's mother stated she had directed the care of Josh with the au pair and was unsure how different it was at nursery.

In first meeting Josh's mother, it became apparent she was quite directive and this initially made me feel quite nervous. She was quite direct about how she wanted his sleep routine to continue with the buggy. We managed to discuss a few areas to support Josh, but I could feel a tense atmosphere when we discussed routines and play opportunities being made a part of that routine, such as stories during rest time.

Once Josh began to attend the baby room, it came to light after a few weeks that Josh had attended a couple of settings previously and his mum hadn't been very happy with them. The settling in process of the previous nurseries had been unsuccessful and she felt she hadn't been listened to. She also said she felt Josh seemed to be crying every time she came to pick him up and felt that the staff were looking at her and making judgments.

During the first few weeks of being in the baby room, Josh's mum was quite defensive in her approach, but I felt this was her anxiety and stress from previous experiences. For me, it actually felt like she was putting Josh's needs first and was really concerned that he had the value and love that she was seeking with others as well as in herself.

During the first two weeks, when Josh was introduced to the baby room, he would move around a lot and became quite bouncy and demanding when his mum spoke to us, sometimes putting his hand over her mouth to quiet her. Josh seemed to be a sociable boy and enjoyed engaging in the play activities and with others.

Reflections of practice

One of the things that we wanted to develop with Josh was to enable him more independence in terms of sleep time. As highlighted, Josh's mother was quite insistent that he continued having daytime sleeps in the buggy, which wasn't very practical in our group care setting. If he was younger perhaps it would have been satisfactory but, because he was 14-months-old and mobile, it was more challenging. Josh also didn't seem to particularly want to go in the buggy during the day. We had to also remind ourselves and his mother that daytime sleep was a lot shorter and different than nighttime sleep. We had to approach this very sensitively with his mother because we didn't want her to feel that she was doing something wrong or inappropriate. We advised her to go back to her health visitor and seek some further guidance about nighttime sleep and we would try a few strategies to support her as well. She seemed to be happy with this discussion around sleep and felt listened to. One of the things that we had to also consider was that sometimes Josh just didn't want to go to sleep. He was happy to be resting but he wasn't keen to sleep, although one of these areas he liked to spend time in was the cushioned corner, near the home play area. After lunch, he would settle down and have a story read to him. He liked flopping down and snuggling into the large beanbags. One of the issues about Josh not sleeping and just resting was that, when his mother picked him up about 6 p.m., he was extremely tired so by the time he got home he had fallen asleep or slept once home. This meant that Josh's mum felt she hadn't had any quality time with him and, if he fell asleep on the way home, she struggled to get him to sleep during the night.

This was quite challenging because we had to negotiate family needs as well as recognize and meet Josh's needs. We also had to consider what we could offer as well as our own experiences in what we thought about sleep time, too. Sometimes our thinking around sleep and rest time may not align with families' attitudes and practices around sleep time. By being in the baby room Josh's needs were met, particularly during rest and sleep time, rather than if we had tried to accept him with the older toddlers.

As the months progressed, we noted that Josh was an independent child and would be a very strong leader with his peers. He also initiated lots of play songs with them. One example of his leadership was when, in the sleeping area, he had placed all the blankets in the middle of the room and was jumping on them and encouraging the others to join in. He was laughing and all the other children were laughing as well, and it resulted in the practitioner laughing too as they had decided that what they were doing was not what we had in mind!

Josh was a popular little boy and the other children warmed to him. His communication was very good, and he was able to articulate his needs well to both his peers and to us. His favorite activity was going on outings and to the local park, and I reflected on whether this was a familiar experience Josh had experienced with his au pair. This seemed to be the highlight of his day, moving beyond the setting. I wondered sometimes whether he felt confined in one room and physically limited in being able to express himself and his physicality. He sometimes got frustrated in the baby room but, when we took him outside to the local park, it was like observing a different child. He really engaged in this space and the play was much more centered around what he wanted to do, and this was interesting to watch as he grew and developed.

Reflective accounts within a Person-Centered Approach

From a PCA, the practitioners were listening to Josh and what his needs were. At 14-months-old, it felt like he had quite a turbulent start in terms of the caregivers around him. His consistency was his mother although, at times, having a new partner meant he was sharing her affection at home in the evenings and at weekends. In this setting, he was assigned to myself but, before me, he had several caregivers and this was challenging for him. It therefore took him quite a long time to trust me and for me also to understand, through his behavior, what he was really feeling. Sometimes what he was showing wasn't always conveying what he was feeling. For example, sometimes he seemed like he was angry with another child and was quite aggressive, but really, he was frustrated with himself and his surroundings, and just needed to have the space to express himself.

The other thing to consider through a PCA, was being empathic towards him as well. As the weeks' progressed Josh was becoming increasingly mobile. He was almost deemed as one of the older members within the baby room and it was important for the practitioners to reflect on what his needs were compared to some of the young infants in the room. He wasn't quite ready to go into the toddler group but physically he was as able as them. Therefore, Josh spent time with the older children outside. This was helpful because it gave him an opportunity to engage with slightly older children. Since Josh attended many hours during the day, he did get very tired, sometimes in the morning. He would want to go and sit on a cushion or a beanbag around 10:30 a.m. and have 45 minutes rest and even sleep then rather than at lunchtime. Again, this was something I shared with his mother and we discussed how were meeting Josh's needs. The changed routine of sleeping earlier was also helpful for his mother as Josh didn't often have a later sleep. Josh's mum therefore had some time with him in the evening before his bath and bed. I was listening to his needs and not what our needs as a baby room organization was going to do for the day as well.

Case study 3
Introduction to the infant

Lisa was 22-months-old when she started attending nursery. She was physically very tall for her age, with long dark hair and was almost ready to be going into the toddler room rather than the baby room. This was a decision that we had to make as a team and, as the group leader, I wanted to observe her before making the final decision about where to place her. If she was going to be in the toddler room, she would be very young in her peer group or, if she was going to be in the baby room, she would be one of the older ones. I talked to her parents as well and both were professionals.

Lisa had very little verbal language; she would vocalize sounds, but she wouldn't really talk much. Her speech was quite difficult to understand and, when I showed the parents around the baby room and the setting, I also noticed that Lisa was walking quite rigidly. She was physically appearing to show physicality of a much younger child and she seemed to be tripping over her feet. I sensitively asked Lisa's parents about her development and if the health visitor had recommended any support or had made any general evaluations. They both said no, stating everything was absolutely fine. They continued to say that she was hitting all the milestones she was supposed to. However, the parents did seem a little defensive in their response. I wasn't convinced or confident in Lisa's speech development but didn't want to make any judgments or presume I knew more. I therefore followed this up later in subsequent weeks with the health visitor and parents, regarding her mobility and her speech.

One of the challenges I had with Lisa was that, because of her parents both being professionals, it felt that they were quite guarded about their daughter in terms of needing any further support and reluctant to approach areas of development. It would have been easy for me to have brushed it over and continued, but it was my duty of care as a professional to ensure I was meeting her needs as an infant and ensuring she was accessing the support she needed. I wondered sometimes whether I was too invested emotionally in her care and felt quite stressed by some of the interactions with the parents. I leaned on my colleagues for support, and they were reassuring and supported my decisions. I was also able to have supervision with my manager, which also helped. I had to also recognize that I wanted it to be a parent partnership and listen to their thoughts about Lisa as much as what we would do in the baby room as well.

Reflections of practice

Messy play was a fascinating area to observe with Lisa. One of the things that she would do regularly was paint using thick brushes that were on offer. There were other brushes, as well as other painting utensils, but she was very free and would frequently go for one type of brush. She would predominantly choose neutral colors. Occasionally, she would paint pictures of specific things and then she would brush them out. She used black and brown paint to brush out her pictures and, once Lisa had finished painting, rather than putting it down she would start to paint her hands and then up her arms. We tried to engage in a conversation with her about this, but it was quite challenging. Lisa didn't seem to want to communicate why she was doing it. We therefore allowed her and accepted it and observed her in the process of panting her arms and the picture, allowing her to engage in her world of play with paint mediums.

What I noted from the process was that she liked the sensation of the cold wet paint on her arms. She also seemed to like the drying effect that it had on her hands too, and she would splay out her fingers and then close them tight as the paint began to slowly dry, creating cracks on her skin. She seemed to like the sensory experience of it all. This wasn't something that she did occasionally, it was an activity that she did quite frequently and generally mid-morning.

Another area that I thought was interesting when I observed Lisa was when we were doing music. We used to create a time to sit down, play instruments and sing songs. It wasn't really a 'circle time' because the babies were just too young, but we did call it 'group song time' and it was just an opportunity for them to engage together in a collective musical time. If the infants didn't want to participate, then we would either take them to settle elsewhere or they could go and play with an alternative activity. Lisa would often come sit down and begin doing the songs but, after a few minutes, found it really challenging to sit still for very long. She would often get up and go do something else instead. She did return quite frequently, which we accepted was part of how she wanted to be in terms of her independence. When we did dance, as part of the music, she tended to join in much more with this and particularly liked the ribbons as part of the music session. She used to wave them around above her hand head and, again, the silky sensation falling on her face seemed to relax her. She would laugh when she danced and, although was quite uncoordinated, she continued to join in. She would topple and, after falling or knocking into something, would resume her dance. We had to ensure there was enough space for her to be able to move freely. From the observations, we noted that she got frustrated with her own lack of physical agility and that she was troubled by not being able to walk in a straight line particularly well. Sometimes she looked like she was going to trip over her own feet, for no specific reason, and this was followed up with further observations and conversations with her parents and professionals beyond the setting. These included speech therapists and occupational therapists regarding her development.

What I did notice through these activities, was her sense of achievement when she was able to do something and accomplish or initiate an activity on her own rather than something that was set by us. I noticed that she got frustrated quite quickly and, again, I think this frustration was within herself about her movement and lack of being able to express herself among her peers. Her concentration was quite sporadic; however, she would wallow during the creative painting and even when she painted her arms and hands, she was immersed in this activity, not really creating anything but just enjoying the process of it.

Reflective accounts within a Person-Centered Approach

From a PCA, one of the things that was important with Lisa was to begin with thinking about where she was, rather than where we thought she should be. We also had team meetings and conversations about whether she would be in the toddler room with slightly older children or whether to remain in the baby room. Lisa wasn't very confident, and I think having an opportunity to be with slightly younger children potentially gave her that confidence, not defined by her chronogical age but rather their personal development.

During her play and engaging in activities, she was more engaged in the process of the activities and this was important for us to observe. We needed to ensure we were refecting on the process rather than having a predetermined outcome when activities were planned. I think this was important because, for her, what she was trying to process was being revealed through play. For her, communication was challenging as well as physically being able to move as quickly as she liked. Supporting what she could do rather than what she couldn't do was therefore about creating lots of space and opportunities for different sensory activities. One of them, for example, was rather than creating a gluing activity (which, of course, many of the infants in the baby room wouldn't be doing anyway) was to put the glue (flour and water) on the table without anything else so she had the medium on the table just to explore. She had stopped mouthing things but did sometimes tend to put things in her mouth. Lisa also got tired at lunch, so we aimed to do a lot of our creative messy play activities in the morning when she was more alert. When she became more tired, we would create different opportunities for her so that she could relax more, and this would be maybe going outside for a walk or engaging with small world play or building bricks or puppets.

Case study 4
Introduction to the infant

Bella was 18-months-old when she started in the baby room. Key specialists working within the local autheducation department asked if we could accommodate Bella and we were happy to do so. Her mum had come from Brazil and Bella did not know English. Her mother spoke a little bit of English but it was very limited. Her mum was attending a course at the local college and was working part time. She lived in a bedsit in the local area, with her own mother (Bella's grandmother). The grandmother came to visit as well but also didn't speak any English. It was the grandmother who would be picking up Bella frequently.

The parents were also vegetarian, and Bella's mum was quite keen for her to have dinners, even though they weren't sure if she was going to be coming at lunchtime. We stipulated when the time for lunch was. We also stated we could probably keep some food for her for a little while but if it was too late, then it may not be very good to eat. This was also quite challenging because we had a set mealtime and some of the staff were worried we would end up feeding the infants all day. We had to think about this together and how this would work in meeting both the family's and our needs regarding mealtimes. Another factor in this family was that Bella's mother was six months pregnant. When I met Bella, she seemed quite insular, held two figures in her hands and didn't give us much eye contact but remained near her mum when she came for settling in times. She had several settling in sessions with her mother before coming herself, and this continued for several weeks.

Reflections of practice

Two areas that I thought were interesting when I observed Bella was during her engagement in 'make believe' time in the home area. This was quite revealing for me in terms of how she cooked her pretend food and 'played home'. She often spoke in her own language and moved about the area, acting as a mum would. She even put teddies up to her and pretended that she was pregnant. Occasionally, she also seemed to take the persona of the grandmother as well and she would talk with figures and dolls and engage with them.

She would never use the table that was available but would often sit on the floor on a cushion and dish out food, or she would draw pictures of the food that she would have and then bring them into the home corner area. Bella didn't shout in the home area but rather talked quietly and seemed quite settled, seemingly wanting to re-play and symbolically act in the home area.

Another area that was interesting was through her singing. Bella seemed to enjoy singing the nursery rhymes and very quickly was able to learn the words for the songs. She was quite receptive to the different songs even though they were quite different to what she was familiar with. Initially, we observed Bella as we sang them. One of the things I wanted to develop in the baby room was to encourage a connection between the home and the family, so I asked her mum if she could bring in and share some songs that they sang at home. She agreed and this was insightful and interesting to observe. When we played her home songs, Bella's whole face lit up and her eyes widened. She leaned her body forward and was clapping her hands, recognizing the songs. She would then continue singing and clapping, smiling at everybody. She seemed to be receiving the songs well and wanted to share her cultural singing with her peers in the group. As practitioners, we joined in with some of the other infants in the room and you could see she was gaining a sense of satisfaction, and she seemed really delighted in the way that she was leading the song time. It gave her an inner strength. Being immersed in a world where she is trying to quickly understand the language and the cultural differences is challenging and, through song, it was now a time when she was leading and taking responsibility of the songs and the space, showing delight in doing so.

Reflective accounts within a Person-Centered Approach

In terms of a PCA, I think about unconditional positive regard for Bella and accepting who she is. It is not just providing her with space to be able to contribute what she wants but also supporting her in gaining a sense of autonomy. As Bella grew more familiar with her surroundings, she would also play with her small people that she brought in on her settling in days as she replayed home life. Role play was a frequent feature when she was in the baby room.

Case study 5
Introduction to the infant

Xander was eight-months-old when he came to the setting for settling in. He was brought in by his father, who was a single parent. His father was very protective of Xander and disclosed that his mum had moved away and had got mental health concerns but wouldn't be a part of his and Xander's life. Another area that was significant was that Xander had been diagnosed with a significant hearing impairment. He had recently been lip reading and signing and were in the process of deciding whether he would be having cochlear implants, At this point, his father was quite anxious and seeking support.

Reflections of practice

In the baby room, we created an environment that we felt would be engaging and supportive of Xander's development and everyday experiences. One of these activities was to include the use of treasure baskets. These contained everyday household items that he could play with. Playing with everyday objects is often replaced with manufactured, commercially appealing toys for specific purposes. However, in recent years there has been a movement in early childhood education and care settings and home contexts, towards reflecting on the impact of plastic waste in our environment. *Loose Parts*, the use of everyday objects found in the environment, has also re-emerged in settings with revitalized interest and developing understanding of how they could be used. For many practitioners, this is a novel approach to play and one less familiar to their own family or educational pedagogy. The treasure basket experience is a valuable approach of allowing a young infant (generally from six months of age) to engage with every day, open-ended items.

Goldschmied and Jackson (1994) approach placed infants at the center of the experience, with a focus on developing the importance of a genuine personal relationship between individual children and their caregiver. A treasure basket can include metal and natural mediums, open-ended resources such as items that, on their own, could be interpreted as anything the imagination allows, such as a stick. The basket experience allows the baby to have a satisfying sensory play experience without interference from an adult. However, the presence of the caregiver remains part of the process and the items should be selected with a consideration of their appropriateness to safety and health precautions. This was something Xander was really drawn to, and he would sit, taking many of the objects in and out. He would mouth them and make noises as he looked to explore, using all his senses. Sometimes we had a few baskets out and other infants would be at theirs as well, and he was always happy for other infants to be part of his play.

While his hearing impairment was significant, he would still make lots of eye contact and would engage with myself and others in the baby room. He would cry if his needs weren't met immediately and, if you were not aware of his hearing impairment, you would have not suspected that he had a hearing loss. His hearing aids were checked and monitored regularly by an external professional. I had many conversations with the professional and she would create six-week targets to really support his development. This was helpful for me as well in terms of engaging with Xander and not trying to do too much for him. For example, we had specific nursery rhymes with cue cards and props that he could engage with to make sense of what we were trying to say. We also had pictorial images for everything and encouraged him to make different sounds using play bubbles. Supporting Xander culminated in using the majority of resources and activities with all the infants because I found visual aids to be beneficial for all the infants in their learning and development.

Xander was very quick at physically moving around although wasn't quite walking when we first met. He didn't tend to pull at his hearing aids and, with the little bit of hearing he had, this obviously helped somewhat.

As well as Xander, we needed to support his dad. He would often be asked where Xander's mum was, and I think sometimes he felt quite awkward about this and was quite a private person. One of the things we wanted to do was encourage dad to be part of nursery life. However, in a predominantly female environment, this can be quite challenging, so we sat down and talked to him about some of the things he likes to do and whether he would like to be part of our community. From this conversation, he decided that he would like to develop the outside garden area with us and started to create a growing area. Even though Xander was only eight-months-old and the garden area was a learning activity for the slightly older children, the infants were encouraged to be part of the growing area. I think this made a big impact, seeing his dad as part of the baby room community and I think it really helped in the relationship between all of us as practitioners and the wider parent community. I was grateful that he was able to give us some of his time. From this role, I noticed he would come into the baby room a lot more and was a lot less intimidated by the environment. He had initially intended to drop Xander off, leave, and then pick him up without too much engagement. But for me, it was important that he was part of the baby room life, as it was an extension of home and family rather than just somewhere offering day care.

Reflective accounts within a Person-Centered Approach

I think with Xander, a PCA for him and his father was about empathizing and not making judgments. Interestingly, some of the staff found it challenging to speak to him as much as he spoke to them. I think they were so used to talking to females that sometimes I had to check myself and think 'ok I need to have a conversation and include fathers more'. As a father who was primarily responsible for Xander's care, I needed to reflect and think about whether I spoke to him differently to the mothers I engaged with. I also needed to consider how my body language was and how I was conveying myself to Xander's dad so that he felt included and part of our baby room community. I was aware not to make judgements about the mother, too. I had been given as much information as he wanted to give and I'm sure there was probably a lot more that I wasn't told but it wasn't for me to make assumptions. It was my role to support Xander and care for him within the baby room. I was conscious I didn't want to be telling his father what to do or distancing the relationship, in an expert-novice relationship, which can often happen, particularly where there's uncertainty about how the professional relationship's going to work.

Case study 6
Introduction to the infants

I was approached by a health visitor about a family who had recently moved to the area wanting to attend the baby room and was happy for them to visit the day nursery I was working in.. The infants were nine-month-old twin boys. When I met them with their mother, I got a sense of why I was approached by the health visitor. She had already approached two other nurseries before me. During the settling in times, the first few weeks the twins, Ashley and Aaron, were babbling to each other and would often roll over each other. Their physical play together was very intense and, at times, quite rough. They were very physical towards each other, almost as if they were one. The mother would often laugh nervously at their behavior and I noticed that she rarely said no to them even when one of the twins would be biting another or pulling their hair. They were quite physical with each other during the settling in period. They were to attend the setting for three to six months before moving again. Their father was currently being investigated for domestic violence and, because it was an open prison, he was able to return to the local area (under supervision) but he wasn't allowed to see the mother.

Reflections of practice

While their physical play was entwinement with each other, I wanted to explore some other areas that they would often do in their play. Within the baby room, they seemed to be very drawn to the sand play and the shredded paper play that we had out in a blow-up paddling pool. This was a continuous provision in the room, and they seemed to be drawn to the sensory play, filling and emptying cups. They liked to empty the paper out of the paddling pool frequently but then put it all back in. They would do this several times and seemed to be drawn to those sensory experiences that had no permanence.

In some ways, this reflected how they felt about where they were as they had moved several times and had observed different things at home. They often played rough and tumble, which would tend to move into rough play; something we had to be mindful in allowing. We also wanted to encourage some separation as the other infants didn't want to be engaged and part of the rough and tumble play. We didn't want to keep saying 'no' to them and being negative, but we also had to be aware that they couldn't keep biting each other, themselves, or another child in the group.

We had to discuss this with the mother as a team and think about strategies that would be helpful. One of the things around this was being clear about distraction and ensuring that they had individual time as well as time together within their baby room experience. In group care, particularly with twins, it would have been easy to have seen them as a collective but it was important that we didn't, particularly in the way they were displaying behavior during this time. Some of the behavior was quite challenging so we had to think about what we were engaging them with and what seemed to be of interest to them. It was interesting to see the patterns of behavior emerging due to their temporary circumstances and how they played. It was during this time that I also had to reflect on the theory of attachment and separation as well as how transitions can impact development.

Reflective accounts within a Person-Centered Approach

I found caring for the twins quite a challenging experience because they were nine-months-old and not quite able to understand what was happening or able to process the circumstances around them. I was also aware that their behavior was reflecting how they were feeling and the anxiety that was occurring within them. Although they were attached to their mother, I think the bonding experience had been disrupted where she had been trying to cope with the father's relationship. Perhaps because there were two of them, they had been left at home for long periods of time to play together. This had created an inseparable bond, but they almost acted as if it was them against their world, finding separation hard, and uncertain about their individual self. Their bond together was a secure base and it felt that having an attachment to each other was significant. Therefore, it was necessary to sensitively carve out some individual time for them to spend with an adult who they could learn to trust and understand as well as being separated for short periods of time so they can make sense of themselves as an individual as well as a twin.

In presenting these case studies, I have illustrated some of the everyday lived experiences of the infants I cared for and how I supported them. This has been illustrated in the engagements with the infants as I cared for them and supported them in developing a sense of belonging in the baby room. Some common areas for consideration that can be drawn from each of them include:

- Knowing the infant
- Understanding child development
- Listening to the parents and creating relationships
- Being authentic in the relationships
- Being available
- Being tuned in
- Being responsive
- Being consistent.

3
A personal approach to a PCA of working ethically with infants

Learning objective

To develop an understanding of the complexities surrounding working within baby room communities and how PCA could support this role.

To begin considering personal feelings and challenges around practice.

In the home and formal day care settings, the close and personalized relationship between caregiver (both parent and practitioner) and infant, can be referred to as intersubjectivity—the secure engagement that occurs between caregiver and infant, as the infant develops an understanding of the society and culture they exist in. Bronfenbrenner (1979) evaluated the contextualized societal surroundings of a developing infant in each place and time as they develop and grow within their cultural environment. Cultural upbringing includes the impact of issues, such as religion and culture, on the developing infant as well as local national and global policies. Bronfenbrenner's theory suggests that infants (and children) and families cannot be understood in isolation but rather within the complex network of society in which they exist. Bronfenbrenner's theory described a model which is presented as a set of eccentric circles, with the micro system at the center, highlighting the closest connections to the infant. As the circles broaden, the social system and social networks of the infant are included and widening still, in which the child is not a direct participant, is the macro system within the model of circles. This includes the broader national social structures, such as education, health, and economic and cultural values, impacting on the infant.

Trevarthen (1993) evaluates that infants are also born as social beings, with the readiness to know another human and engage with them. He evaluated interactions between caregivers as being mutual, with infants able to take the lead within the interaction rather than just responding to their caregiver's lead behavior. Through a turn-taking interaction, the caregiver can adapt their interactive behavior to the rhythms of their infant and encourage them to lead the interaction. These early exchanges have been termed as 'proto conversations'. The patterns of turn-taking includes mutual attention, changes in movement, and smiling, and these early interactions have been regarded as embodying the essentials of the relationship and the communication between caregiver and infant. Observational studies of mother's facial expressions have been historically carried out, for example with Tronik et al's (2005) 'still face' experiment. This

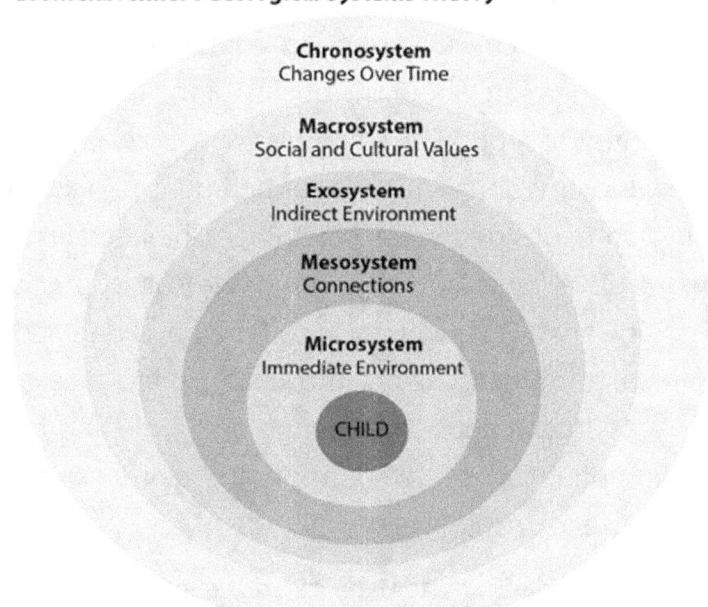

Figure 3 Bronfenbrenner's ecological systems theory.

experiment revealed how infants are capable of initially taking the lead with their parent in the interaction: observing, initiating, and responding to facial cues as they interact. However, if the parent does not respond and the infant consistently fails to receive a response from their caregiver, when they attempt communication, they will resign into silence. They will eventually stop trying to initiate the communication knowing that they will not be responded to. This confirmed the notion that infants will seek a caregiver's attention to interact and communicate with them (Brazelton, 1990).

Another relevant key figure in thinking about the importance of relationships, is the work of Brazelton (1990) and his concept of joint action: being contingent and reciprocal. It is about how the caregiver and infant continually influence each other. It is therefore about the quality of the relationship, not just quantity of arousal and stimulation that was significant to develop emotionally and for attachment to occur. By introducing and considering these eminent pioneers in the file of infant development and learning, we can appreciate that communication is, therefore, a collaborative interactive process, such as mutual gazing into each other's face and using gestures. Interactions also change over time and have the power to influence the relationship and gain a sense of self within the relationship.

In a day nursery, working in the baby room, we introduced baby signing. This became a fun and interesting way to develop nursery rhymes and song time. What the staff had not anticipated was that, by observing and responding to the infants through baby signs, they were understanding the infants' needs better and the infants were communicating more effectively. The baby signing approach was adopted as a way of tuning into the infants, allowing them to initiate the lead. I was often asked for milk by a child signing to me. The sign for 'sorry' and 'more' were also ways the infants communicated their needs to me. By developing the approach together, both the practitioners and the infants were interacting and learning the signs together, developing a close relationship. The practitioners no longer associated being 'bored' when working with the infants or wishing they had more interactions—they were observing so many ways to communicate together!

How do I care for infants and what is my position and influences?

Attachment is the emotional process arising from innate behavior and a biological control system that drives this behavior. Attachment theory has predominantly focused on infants' relationships to a primary caregiver and Bowlby's (1953) theory offers the view that infants are born with an innate biological need to create secure, close relationships critical for survival. Bowlby cites an increase in adverse mental health outcomes when infants experience separation from their prime caregiver, stating they need consistent physical closeness, a secure base. If this is not achieved, then separation anxiety may occur. Furthermore, the importance of nurturing needs being met is critical in the first two years and provides the healthy foundations for later development. The strong affection infants feel for close adults in their lives leads to feelings of pleasure through interactions and being comforted during times of stress. Though subsequent research has evaluated infants' ability to create bonds with multiple attachment figures, including Rutter (2002) who disputed the dependency on the monotropic figure, emphasis, for him, was about focusing on the quality of care to healthy developing relationships. Similarly, Schaeffer and Emerson (1964) also evaluated that infants were able to achieve multiple attachments by ten-months-old, emphasizing it was the responsiveness and quality of the interaction that determined the primary and complementary attachment figures. However, the ethological theory, developed by Bowlby (1969), remains a widely accepted view of attachment. Belsky et al (2007) further developed understandings of attachment and added that it was about the evolving care of relationships over time and are context-dependent, not simply a static single or stable relationship. I feel this resonates well with Dunn (1994), who also evaluated primary caregiver bonding experiences and found that this was dependent on the age and changes as the infant becomes more independent. However, while attachment is conceived as being fluid, primary attachments remain advantageous to emotional resilience and regulation as more complex understandings about relationships are developed.

Bowlby described the internal images or maps that are built up because of these exchanges as internal working models (IWMs). These internal working models enable the baby to anticipate and interpret the behavior of other people and to plan a response. Where the caregiver is experienced as a source of security and support, the baby develops internal working models in which they have a positive self-image and in which other people are depicted as being trustworthy and responsive. Infants with non-attuned or abusive caregivers, internalize a less positive self-image as being unworthy of love and without agency; they also represent others as unpredictable, unresponsive, and untrustworthy.

Trevarthen (2001) agreed emotions are central to the formation of early relationships and they are continually reacting and adjusting during interactions. Vorria (2003) also examined the quality of attachment and evaluated that a child's capacity for attachment was related to the responses of their caregivers (Nutbrown and Page, 2013). The concept of mind mindedness is the caregivers' ability or willingness to represent their likely thoughts and feelings to who they are caring for. The outcomes of success are deemed to be related to the security of attachment and theory of mind. By responding in a way that shows understanding, reflective function occurs. This is the caregiver's capacity to understand the infant's behavior in terms of internal feeling states. Reflective function is linked to 'maternal parenting' behaviors, such as flexibility and responsiveness, although this extends to all, including those beyond the home, who develop close relationships with the baby and create a safe base. Reflecting on the types of interactions and responses offered, results in the balance between not being too intrusive or passive. This is important because it strikes a balance in an appropriate way and later fosters security in attachments.

An example of this in practice was when I read about Suzanne Zeedyk's work on front-facing buggies and the uncertainty and challenges the child may face when out in the 'external world' rather than their caregivers when visiting unfamiliar places and spaces. As a group caring for infants, myself and my team often took children and infants out on walks and visits to places as part of their setting experience. However, I hadn't really connected the significance to attachment and security with this when the infants and young children couldn't physically see us as we pushed them along. Zeedyk (2008) studied forward facing buggies and found that infants exhibited increased cortisol levels when orientated away from their mother's face, describing how they became emotionally impoverished as their subtle cues to communicate were overlooked when placed in unfamiliar environments with fewer opportunities for interaction. These findings were later confirmed by Blaiklock (2013), who observed that when infants were transported in buggies faced forward, they could not see their parents, and this made interactions more difficult. I hadn't really considered this during unfamiliar walks and surroundings, assuming the infant was quietly happy and settled, but looking out from their buggy was perhaps the infant feeling overwhelmed and quite anxious. We therefore decided to purchase some buggies that faced the adults pushing them, and I noted that this made a difference to how they responded when out on walks. They were certainly more verbal and interactional with me, and it provided a further opportunity to extend our bond away from the setting. These two studies suggested buggies that face towards a parent will provide more opportunities for parents to interact with their children, and thereby help to facilitate language development, to secure healthy attachment, and reduce infant stress levels (parents being physically and emotionally available).

What is my ethical position and how do I draw on this in framing how I work in the baby room?

Bowlby (1969 p. 77) evaluated how infants and children's mental health were positively impacted 'through warm, intimate and continuous relationships with the mother or mother substitute'. The inclusion of 'substitute' (Bowlby, 1969 p. 77) has significance for early years professionals, as while they are not (in many cases) the primary caregiver, they are a supplementary figure who can create secure attachments with babies and young children that promote positive outcomes for those in their care. Bowlby stated that government provision of young children's welfare should not just be focused on inside of the family but others outside of the family, too (Bowlby, 1969 p. 184). In a secure attachment, adult caregivers can provide a safe base for children from which they can explore and learn and where they can return to, as necessary, for reassurance. Infants need validation to feel good about themselves with adults. If they are not paid attention to and their needs or feelings are not listened to, they can feel emotionally rejected. This can potentially, and unintentionally, happen by practitioners who may not know how to support or meet the infants needs emotionally when working with them.

The ethics of care

Taggart (2014, p. 6) recognized the moral aspect of care as a practitioner, especially those working with infants in nursery contexts. Care is conceived as being guided by the practitioners own guiding principles and, for Taggart, greater recognition and discourse needs to be shared and challenged as part of professionalism. When the ethics of care is considered as framing the practitioner's professional role, then discourse about compassion, love, and connectivity come to the fore professionally as opposed to a role which is often viewed as domestic and personal. This chapter does not specifically draw on a singular viewpoint of ethics but rather introduces the concepts and complexity associated with care. In training programs, Taggart (2014 and 2016) argues that training programs should include the ways in which compassion is visible and conceptualized in developing thinking about ethical care, rather than focusing on instrumental outcomes based on the patriarchal view of female suitability that currently exists. Ethics of care certainly raises questions about the emotional involvement in paid employment as well as the complexities of caregiving in forming close emotional relationships. By considering this within a PCA, we need to consider how we work ethically with infants.

I certainly have wrestled with this throughout my professional career and, ethically, I was often challenged by the care I was offering to the infants, the parents requests and anxieties, as well as being able to work and then tune out my professional role once outside of my work. For me, the role as senior lead in the baby room was more than a job, it was a vocation. However, the infants were not my responsibility in the evenings or weekends, and I had to manage the stress and concerns about the infants I was responsible for when they were not at the setting. As a lead, I had to learn to 'let go' and ensure I looked after myself emotionally, too. As I became a parent, I think this created further complexities in having an appreciation of how the parents felt, and I could understand how my caring approaches were ethically considered. An example of how this was challenged was with a parent who was pregnant and had a child already attending the setting. The infant was diagnosed with a genetic disorder and the mother was needing support and care. She had booked her infant into the setting but was now unsure about whether this would be feasible. Through conversations, I had to ensure she made the decision rather than me advising her on what decision should be made. I wanted the parent to not make any quick decisions and thought, if it was me, I would want to give up work. However, it was not for me to say what I would do or make judgments. I had to consider how to be supportive but also ethical in listening and empathizing with the parent.

Taggart (2014) therefore presented an argument for recognizing the moral aspect of care as a practitioner, especially those working with infants in early childhood education and care (ECEC) day nursery contexts. Care is conceived as being guided by the practitioner's guiding principles and, for Taggart, greater recognition and discourses needed to be shared and challenged as part of professionalism. When the ethics of care is considered as framing the practitioner's professional role, then discourse about compassion, love, and connectivity come to the fore professionally. The word 'love' recently gained attention in the way practitioners reflect on their experiences with the infants they're paid to care for, known as Professional Love (Page, 2017). The term, Professional Love, is often interconnected with terms such as early childhood care, affection, and empathy; understanding in articulating feelings towards an infant (Cousins, 2017). In forming close and loving relationships, familiarity, pattern, and predictability of caregiver responses give infants a sense of self. Continuity of attention from key people who know infants and young children well, who are interpreting and responding to their gestures and cues, enable children to attend to their inclinations and to play freely. This is known as 'tuning in'. Tuning in can be helpful in unexpected ways, because they often express emotions that are challenging to manage but, with the support of the key person, they can share their feelings. Tuning in can also be advantageous as a reflection tool for key persons to acknowledge those infants who may be expressive and more insular in conveying their emotions. Infants behavior toward caregivers' responses is therefore critical in helping caregivers appreciate their own behavior when working in the baby room.

Pat, a new practitioner at the setting I was leading, commented on how quick and efficient she was at changing diapers. She was talking about how speedy she was and, with practice, was able to clean the babies in her care without too much resistance and wriggling. Later, during the team meeting, with supervisors and practitioners we discussed how we offered respect during cleaning and supporting infant personal care. I, as the lead supervisor asked the following of the team:

- *Next time you change a diaper, stop and think about the activity. Are you telling the baby what you are doing and going to do?*
- *Are you making eye contact and responding, or leading the talk?*

I asked them to reflect on their facial experiences as practitioners and consider what messages they are conveying when cleaning an infant. Is it a rushed event or an opportunity for qualitative one-on-one time at a slower pace?

All these things remind us that connecting does not just happen with educational learning activities but in everyday actions.

Figure 4 and Figure 5 Part of everyday interactions with the infants we care for.

Figure 4 and Figure 5 (continued)

How does this all connect with a PCA? A person-centered educational space

Childhood, specifically in the UK and beyond, is considered an important and unique period regarding their emotional regulation. Rogers (1951) maintained that individuals have the capacity to become who they want to be with the support of others who genuinely care and try to understand them. Being unconditionally accepted within supportive environments where children are assumed to be trustworthy, resourceful, and capable of developing a self-understanding and direction. A PCA therefore encourages the natural expression of warmth, loyalty, and trustworthiness within relationships, listening and accepting a person's individuality. Authentic relationships are built, and the core conditions can be fostered to provide positive change for children. The practitioners are attuned to the emotional and social needs of infants and young children enabling them to increase their self-understanding, self-appreciation, and self-confidence as they begin to understand, appreciate, and trust others. There are various factors that predict the development of self-regulation in young children. The first is a strong attachment to primary caregivers or, as PCA refers to as, "unconditional positive regard" from the adults in their lives. In other words, practitioners who are emotionally available to the infant and not caring in a way that is not directed by the infant's behavior. By being emotionally available and professionally loving towards the infant in their care, they are offering opportunities for them to face challenges and take risks in a safe and emotionally holding environment. In nurturing this emotional and physical space, infants then develop agency of voice and can take the lead in their own behavior. By allowing infants to take and manage risks, they're able to become independent and resilient, supported through 'co-regulation' with practitioners who are also nurturing towards them. This can range from talking calmly to the infant to allowing freedom of choice within the play offered.

An example of this was within the baby room whereby a a sensory space was created in an area of the room for the infants to freely play and engage in. We often organized the room so it was appealing to the adult's eye but, perhaps, less accessible at times for the infant to engage in. On another rainy day, we decided to bring in some of what we considered to be the outdoor equipment and use it in the space inside. We had a slide, some hoops, a paddling pool (filled with balls), and large wooden blocks. All these resources were often stored and kept outdoors but, when we talked about it as a team, we asked each other "why?" Having brought in the equipment, we noticed the confidence and the risks the infants were taking. Knowing they could land on carpet, they explored much more than they did outside and were also negotiating the space with each other. They were also interacting with each other and using their whole bodies going in the hoops and moving them around the room. The session was valuable in our role as practitioner by thinking about how we assumed children play, but also about the resources we assume should be outdoors or fit for purpose in a particular space.

Within this framework, the focus is on caring communities and how this has and can be enhanced though play pedagogies with a focus on emotions.

A Person-Centered Approach (PCA) to a CRIB of Care
Baby room relationships in formal day care

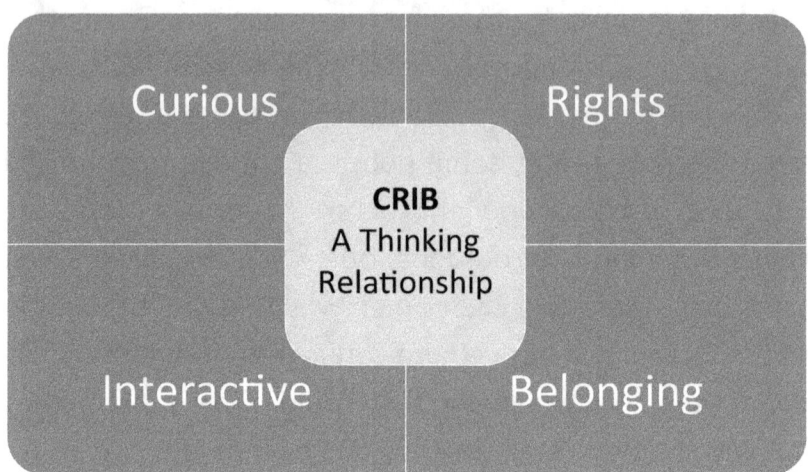

A Person-Centered Approach (PCA) to a CRIB of Care
Baby room relationships in formal day care

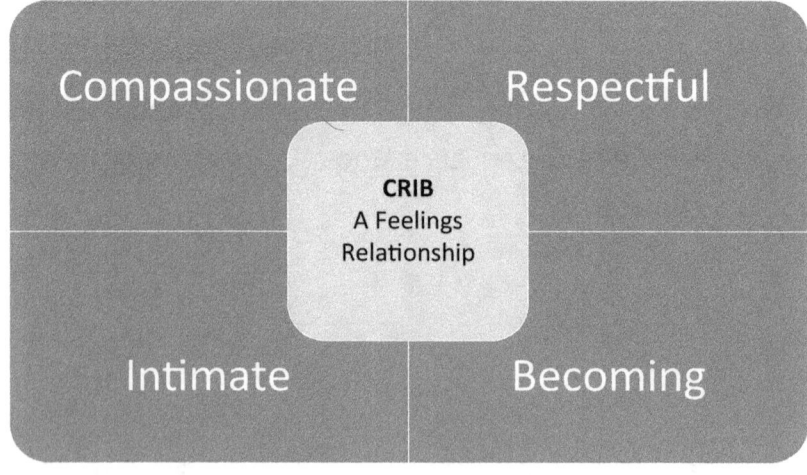

Creating Person-Centered caring communities in formal early years education and care settings

The focus of this chapter is on how caring communities and opportunities of practitioner's personal growth can become part of the baby room. Philosophically, early childhood educators provide infants with opportunities to consider themselves beyond their behavior. Infants with varying personalities need to feel welcome and comfortable. This encourages them to be open to new experiences, learn new things, and find new ways to invest in themselves. They may also demonstrate trust in themselves by believing that they can do something, using and orchestrating their own direction and process within their everyday experiences. Practitioners provide interactive experiences that demand more action orientation, such as blowing bubbles, coloring, or sharing thoughts and feelings about their life events. These types of experiences are a necessary part of early childhood learning because they provide opportunities for infants to gain sensory experiences of the world around them and the joy the feel. In all the activities available and engaged in over time, they can discern what is enjoyable and comforting for them as well as what is safe and socially appropriate, and they learn to actualize these positive experiences for themselves. Rogers (1961) believed that creating rapport creates a safe and welcoming environment and facilitates the individual's courageous acceptance of self and the respectful acceptance of others.

As researcher and practitioner, I have been very fortunate for the opportunities to reflect and observe the way pedagogy has been approached with infants through an "edu-care" approach (Gerber, 2003). Pedagogy is not only about the how and the why of what early year's educators do in their professional roles. It also extends to the way educators engage with the expectations presented to them in their work setting and, in this context, the baby room. Infants learn best in atmospheres that provide a stimulating and prepared environment where they learn from their own perspectives. In the setting, time to plan areas for children to engage with their emotions and be cared for by a listening and observant practitioner is essential for development and wellbeing to occur. Aligned to some of Rogers' principles, Gerber (2003) considered respect as the basis of an edu-caring approach, demonstrating respect every time we interact with them. Respecting a child means treating even the youngest infant as a unique individual:

- An Authentic Child: An authentic child is one who feels secure, autonomous, competent, and connected.
- Trust in the infant's competence: We have basic trust in the infant to be an initiator, to be an explorer and eager to learn
- Sensitive observations: To observe carefully to understand the infant's communications and their needs during the day.

The more we observe, the more we understand and appreciate the enormous amount and speed of communication, and how learning is communicated in the many forms of communication infants may use. An understanding of this enables the practitioner to listen to and communicate with children to gain an appreciation and better understanding of their emotions. Listening and recognizing children's emotions therefore become more than a simple interactional engagement and can be shown through their creativity, behavior, or how they use hand gestures.

It requires reflections on the part of the practitioner about their own emotional state as well and the communicative approaches they use. Interpreting language and language as part of a complex chain of utterances; emphasizing the unique meanings an infant may bring to the understanding. Through parental sharing, an understanding to language beyond the immediate context is also made and understood with the idea of working towards a feeling of self-satisfaction rather than conforming to an external success managed by others. Rogers points out that this is about self-actualization needs. Self-actualization is a person's instinctive need, and it is the most important inner motility, even the power to promote the society. The aim of education is to promote "selfhood"; to be realized. Therefore, self-actualization becomes the basic education aim and Rogers emphasizes that the aim of education is to foster open-minded, dynamic, and adjustable people who know how to learn and continue to learn (Maslow, 1962).

4
A community of practice: PCA supervision in the baby room

This chapter focuses on the value of a PCA during supervision and in planning and supporting a practitioner's development. A Person-Centered Approach (PCA) includes how we view, listen to, and support a person based on their strengths, abilities, aspirations, and preference to make decisions to maintain a life which is meaningful to them. Person-centered thinking can therefore be helpful when considering, planning, organizing, understanding, and connecting with communities. A Person-Centered Approach (PCA) can therefore be a useful way to approach supervision with team members of early years communities.

Learning objectives

To develop an understanding of valuing supervision as a listening approach within PCA.

To begin considering personal feelings and challenges around practice and how communication and supervision can be a way of planning and equipping yourself with strategies and support.

Person-centered supervision and planning emphasizes the importance of reflective practice that has become a regular part of the everyday work. Practitioner's reflective practice includes observing, evaluating, and communicating with each other. As a team, in group supervision, these practices can be discussed and, in coming together, provides a helpful way of supporting each other, facilitated by a senior lead. Emphasizing the intrinsic value motivation to successfully work together can also be applied at different levels when working in the baby room. Practitioners often work for long hours, caring for infants and, inevitably, tensions between staff can often arise and a way of managing emotions range from outbursts or, more often, a tendency to hide personal thinking and mask how they feel, fearing they may seem unprofessional or challenged if they do not comply to procedures in the baby room.

Person-centered thinking

In the baby room, the practitioners' work is centered on the close relationships formed with the infants they care for. Heidegger (1990) argued that it is essential to be authentic and consider areas, such as the meanings of individual relationships, emotional engagement, knowledge, and how decision-making occurs, when the baby room team engage with each other. A PCA guides us towards the most appropriate approach for action and recognizes the interconnectedness of individual relationships and how they can flourish. However, it also important to recognize that a PCA requires commitment from each individual to engage, think, and care about how relationships occur with each other as they work together.

Figure 6 Supervision meetings.

The distinction between appraisals and supervision

When I initially worked in the baby room, we would aim to organize monthly appraisals, to discuss job contracts, salaries, promotions, and areas such as leave. The appraisal meetings tended to be formal, and I would often discuss the appraisee's professional development and position within the organization. We completed forms prior to meeting and these often framed what was going to be discussed.

We also introduced buddy group meetings to compliment the appraisals and promote positive peer relationships. The buddy meetings were generally held between peers and were approached like a coaching or mentoring relationship. They were helpful because they supported practitioners in sharing their experiences working in the baby room, providing them with another opportunity to communicate any worries or successes that they would like to develop. This would be areas such as leading a music session or wanting to organize a trip out of the setting, such as going for a local walk with the infants in their care.

Supervision, another form of meeting, and one which is the focus of this chapter, is where the focus is much more on supporting practice and supporting the practitioners in their role of caring for infants. The process of supervision is defined as the interpersonal interaction with the general aim being that one person (the supervisor) meets with another (the supervisee) to help make and develop effective practice. Therefore, supervision in the baby room is about connecting with the practitioners about themselves and how they care for the infants.

Supervision in the baby room I worked at was an opportunity for creating space with a focus predominantly on reflection and development. This is about the daily work practitioner's carry out with the infants they care for but it's also about their thoughts generally and their role and position within the baby room. The supervision meeting could be considered an extension to the buddy meeting, but there is more of an emphasis on the emotional and trusting space so that the supervisee can talk honestly and authentically about their practice as well as themselves within the position of where they work.

Supervision is there for both personal and self-development, and it is an opportunity to offer positive feedback as well as constructive criticism, but it also addresses areas such as confidence and honesty.

Supervision should be conducted within an ethical framework of mutual respect, with both parties contributing to the meeting, thinking about beliefs and values which shape their early practices. These are then grounded in an ethics of care for children and their families working within the setting.

To explain this further, I will share an example of a supervisory meeting I had with a new member of staff. The new member of staff had been attending this setting for about five months and had a group of three children between one or two years of age in the baby room. From the beginning of her employment, she was quite quiet and hesitant in her everyday practice, although there was a sense that she had a caring nature and was able to empathize with the infants in her care. The small group of infants she looked after were regularly observed and she frequently followed their routine, asking questions where necessary about feeding and the changing of diapers.

One of the areas I had noted in her practice, was her reluctance to talk to the parents of the infants she cared for. We had a daily family book containing forms that the parents would take home so they would write anything that had happened differently during the night before returning them the following morning. The main purpose of the book was to discuss any issues or concerns from the previous night, and I found this invaluable because each night could be very different. The infants were very young and there was generally always something written in the books, even if it was just the parents wanting to reassure that all had been well or they had not slept very long, had not fed very much, or had gotten up particularly early. As the lead practitioner, I found it to be really helpful information to get a sense of how the infant would be during the day and how we could support them best in their care.

I had noticed that often the books were placed on the table by the parents and the new practitioner would smile and meet the parents but wouldn't say very much and certainly wouldn't initiate any conversations about the previous night. She also 'disappeared' during the transition of the infants coming into the setting or busied herself, so the more senior practitioners often took the lead with welcoming the family into the setting. The new practitioner would often stand back as well and, although would show a welcoming smile, she often allowed others to take the lead in this process.

During the supervisory meeting, we chatted about practice and areas she thought she had developed well in her time of being in the setting. One of the areas I explored with her was her confidence in talking to parents. It became apparent in our discussion that this was an area she was unfamiliar with. In her previous role, she had tended to follow a work pattern within the time that the parents would drop off and pick up their children, so she did not actually see them very often. She disclosed that she felt awkward, worried they were going ask her something that she wouldn't be able to answer.

She said that she read the handover books every day and found the information helpful but, in speaking to the parents, felt inhibited about what to ask or how to take the lead. We discussed ways this could be supported and how she could do some observing of the more senior practitioners in the room in gaining confidence and thinking about the types of questions and conversations she could initiate with the parents. We also thought about CPD (Continuing Professional Development) opportunities as space where the practitioner could reflect about working with parents and what key things would be helpful. Another area we thought may help, was taking on a responsibility in terms of the parent partnership file. The aim of this was to get a sense of why it is important to talk to families and being inclusive. She seemed quite keen to do this and, within the parenting file, there was the policy practices and everyday ideas and staff meeting comments in terms of how we could support parents in various ways. Being able to read through the parent partnership policy again, enabled her to recognize the values, beliefs, and mission statements we were pursuing within the setting. In the baby room, we aimed to promote joint relationships with the families, to be nurtured and developed together.

One of the targets we decided to outline was enabling the new practitioner to initiate conversations with one of the parents. Initially, she would be supported by senior practitioners, but we also encouraged the senior practitioners to—rather than stepping in—be the person to stand back and allow a little bit more space and time for the new practitioner to have a conversation

Supervision sessions were helpful in terms of thinking about ways we could support the practitioner and enhance her practice through observation and evaluations. We were able to set specific objectives that we both agreed to. Supervision meetings are therefore an opportunity to offer positive feedback as well as constructive criticism about their performance. It highlights training needs and advice regarding professional development. It addresses issues in confidence and honesty when reflecting on their role. Supervision should be a reflective dialogue, and this is an ongoing process with practitioners gathering evidence through their observations and evaluating their practice within the collaborative conversations. The dialogue facilitates professional learning, understanding, and practice because they offer opportunities for sharing insights, exchanging information, constructing knowledge, gaining understanding, and exploring roles and responsibilities. It also reduces the isolation for practitioners by offering the time to connect over their practice and reflect on new possibilities (Rodd, 2013, p. 167).

In creating supervision meetings, it was helpful to focus on the practitioner's everyday practice and the infants that they worked with. Supervision provided the opportunity and space to share how practitioners felt within their roles and how we could support them as a team (Norman, 2022a).

By creating regular supervision meetings, it was more effective and less exhausting to separate supervisory meetings from appraisal meetings rather than combining the two together as one meeting. The need to have supervision meetings for the practitioner's emotional wellbeing was highlighted in Elfer's (2007) studies, who evaluated that working with young children brought an emotional cost. Ward et al (2012) also suggested that a way of supporting that emotional labor of the practitioners in caring emotionally for the infants as part of their paid role, is to ensure that regular supervision occurs. I think this is particularly true for those working in the baby room where the infant's development is rapidly changing, almost daily, and their care needs are aligned with the family's needs as well as thinking about how to create and facilitate educational and play opportunities for them (Norman, 2022b).

Group supervision

Group supervision can also be successful alongside the one-on-one supervisory meetings discussed above. These can be held between practitioners working together or it could be a combination of those less experienced with those more experienced. It would continue to have a supervisor facilitating the session with the main purpose and function of supervision (aligning to my play therapy background) being about providing a space to think about education and being supportive. It is about providing regular space to reflect on the content and practices in their work. It's also about developing an understanding of each practitioner's skill set and how they can enhance them. It is also about deepening and connecting, understanding child development and making connections to the individual children they are working with, creating a space to develop ideas. The creation of opportunities for supervision recognition and validation as a professional, can be enhanced with supervisors supporting supervisees in developing key skills and expertise. The supervisory group model is often where a small group of practitioners, usually at a similar stage of professional development, meet with the supervisor. Alternatively, groups could be made up of both inexperienced and experienced staff and find the model of supervision beneficial because they work in a specific room together or with a specific age range. The supervision involves the objective observations of a colleague's practice, without making interferences, interpretations, or assumptions about their interactions, and then sharing and discussing these observations together as a group. The practitioners may also contribute to the process by sharing observations they have made of children and what they have noted in their development and learning, as well as reflecting on their own practice. Relationships are based on mutual trust and respect, with the supervisors as leaders sharing supervisory responsibilities with the team to ensure that the group possess the necessary professional knowledge and communication skills to manage a task, as well as the willingness to request outside help if a problem is identified and beyond the resources of the group (Rodd, 2013, p 170). It is also about enhancing development to reflect and share constructive and positive feedback as well as critical feedback. Generally, there would be a contract drawn up and recordings made of what happened, what took place during the supervision meeting, and agreements between both parties will be documented. A commitment and responding to a mutual responsibility are a central process of supervision.

Working in the baby room can be highly stressful and often cause burnout with the practitioners dealing with the infants. Part of trying to overcome this as a form of protection, is when practitioners distance themselves and contain their emotions and almost switch off, so they are not as attuned as they could be. There may be comments made referring to working in the baby room as being quite boring or not being much to do. For me, this suggests a distance and anxiety about caring for infants.

By discussing these areas in supervision, practitioners gain a deeper insight into how they are interacting with the infants, really observing them in shaping how they can support them. Supervision is an opportunity to provide space to solve problems and, for me, should be embedded in all settings. Supervision is a great opportunity for practitioners to raise worries and concerns about the infants in their care and their families as well. It is about thinking of challenging situations and overcoming these through communicating different areas of practice and providing support. Communication therefore enables practitioners to organize their feelings and develop, adding value to the care they are providing. Promoting a better, high-quality service supervision can also ensure policies and practices are aligned in meeting the standards expected when working with infants. Supervision is therefore about listening, collaborating, and togetherness in an effort of creating emotional wellbeing of both the infant and practitioners, with positive relationships and enabling environments.

Approaching supervision in a PCA way

A PCA is about discovering and acting on what is important to the individual. It is concerned with continually listening and learning from the person we are engaged with. It is also about focusing on what is most important in the current situation they're working in, as well as their future, and being able to support them through this. Within a PCA, supervision is primarily focused on listening. Creating a space for mutual respect and trying to reduce the power relationships often found with senior members of staff and practitioners working together is important for the baby room. This helps to create options for reflective listening, collaboration, and together teams, connecting with everyone in meaningful ways.

Approaching supervision: listening

Listening in person-centered supervision involves sincere and authentic attention and intention. Attention to the supervisees body language, words, meaning, inspirations, and aspirations is important because it is about findings ways to connect with them. Listening with intention and attention is important to create conditions that give practitioners a voice, so they feel heard and listened to.

Approaching supervision: a collaboration

This is focused on reducing the power dynamics of relationships and the challenges existing between supervisor and supervisee. A PCA focuses on working with people rather than disempowering them by doing things for or to them.

Approaching supervision

Listening alone is insufficient and a clear intention with objectives are helpful in moving forward. Responsive action involves clarity and actions to be practiced because of sharing thoughts within the supervisory meetings.

Figure 7 and Figure 8 Through supervision we reflect on the environment and create outdoor spaces for the babies that are interactional and fun.

An example of a supervision session

Effective supervisors include direction for further professional development, and these include:

- Expertise in the knowledge and skills of professional values and attitudes relevant for the early childhood profession;
- The ability to share knowledge and skills;
- Communication skills and responding to appropriate feedback;
- Involve all the team in various ways;
- Monitoring practitioners progress on a regular basis;
- Having confidence and being receptive to new ideas; and
- Flexible and accessible to staff in their team.

Figure 7 and Figure 8 (continued)

Working within a PCA, the supervisor's attitude, motivation, autonomy, and previous experience are all essential for the supervision sessions to be successful. Supervisors, in their role as leader, should be open, respectful, and collaborative. They should be able to encourage practitioners to move beyond their own basic understanding of concepts and practices to a more sophisticated way of thinking and approaching ideas. A developing ability to analyze, synthesize, and evaluate is all part of becoming a reflective practitioner.

The National Day Nurseries Association (NDNA) (2022) recommends that supervision is an ongoing process, but the need for meetings to discuss observations and feedback depends on the policies and the needs of the individual. Supervisions allow you to:

- *make sure that all children in the nursery are being supported and that there are no concerns.*
- *share success.*
- *provide support for team members around any issues or concerns.*
- *ensure any issues and concerns are solved or supported.*
- *identify any need for further support and encourage staff to identify these needs for themselves* (ndna.org, np).

Supporting the supervisors

As part of a supervision meeting between the senior practitioner and manager, the manager wanted to discuss how the four colleagues were collaboratively working together in the baby room. There had previously been conversations between the staff about managing the infant's behavior, especially the age group between 14 months and two years of age. They were also unsure about responding to the crying infants who ranged from six- to 14-months-old. It seemed some practitioners were struggling with the noise level and becoming stressed, leaving myself as the lead to deal with the crying and behavior or delegating roles. My manager wanted to discuss group care and self-soothing but also support me in my role leading the practice. I was aware of the manager's thoughts but did not want to advocate self-soothing, as I believed the infants needed to be cuddled and responded to immediately, where possible. My approach was to encourage and advocate individualized care within the group setting and encourage the practitioners to respond to the crying positively rather than getting stressed with the noise level.

We approached the complexities around supporting infants and discussed the issues together. The manager, colleagues, and I. Central to this was also ensuring the infant's voices were also included in the discussion and their care.

By creating a group supervision meeting, we developed and wrote up a set of shared actions to be put into place. We thought about positive outcomes for the infants. Working as a collective isn't always about having easy conversations and some of these can be challenging in terms of personal thoughts and experiences about caring for infants. One of the key things that the group did in their supervisory meeting was to bring out the policy of working with infants and reflect and review whether this needed to be updated in terms of how they wanted to support the infants in their care.

Carl Rogers (1970) proposed that individuals are relational, affected by their social and cultural norms. Rogers believed that when we are surrounded by sharp criticism and judgement, individuals are forced to resort to all kinds of strategies to achieve approval and positive regard for themselves. This may result in relying on external authorities for guidance as an attempt to please everyone. This may also result in unpredictable, inconsistent, and incongruent behavior. By offering group supervision, according to Louis (2020), this enables a process of continual and rigorous professional learning in early education as a way of guiding and supporting developing practice. Supervision encourages reflection about daily observations while being offered opportunities to enhance development and awareness of how children learn. The purpose of supervision is to improve operational practice, focusing on how practitioners discuss children's development and learning, interests, and needs, as well as their relationships, in a safe supportive environment (p. 62).

Supervision therefore focuses on :

- Encouraging listening and talking;
- Space to develop and understand play and the reasons why children behave the way they do;
- Members of the team feeling less recognized and developing low morale if they are unable to process and share their experiences looking after and educating children;
- Creating space for supervision leaders and practitioners so that they can explore difficult issues and talk, make suggestions, and seeking help; and
- Promoting ongoing self-understanding, self-awareness, and a commitment to learning about themselves (Louis, 2020).

By engaging in group communication, it is a shared commitment to the valuable and respectful way of interacting with each other. By connecting with each other, it develops a sense of depth, intensity, and relatedness of the dialogue. Including a PCA also includes considering and discussing anxieties and reluctance in areas of their role. By being empathic together, the communication is centered on the process rather than a state in entering the private world of another person's values, views, and beliefs. In sharing and showing empathy, more can be understood about each other and communities can be developed. Mearns and Thorne (2000) discuss the importance of cultivating a cherishing and affirming relationship with the self, assisted with the help of another person. It is also important to recognize that no two people experience things in the same way. If we truly want to understand our supervisees experience, we must actively listen to their narrative. On a practical level, in the baby room, many of these areas can be met through active listening, as supported by Rogers, but also the value of observation.

Including observations as part of supporting supervision and practice

Knowing how to observe can be one of the most rewarding and yet challenging aspects of practitioner's role. Initially, those engaged in training may view observations as an add-on to their practice, with little connection to how they plan or evaluate children's development. Reflection and discussion about what were observed between practitioners are valuable in developing knowledge and understanding about children. This includes how practitioners could support children's development and improve communities of practice through observations.

Figure 9 Treasure basket play.

Several years ago, I delivered a project over the course of a six-week period, with a colleague I was supervisor for within a nursery setting.

The project included organizing a weekly session, lasting about half an hour. We selected a range of equipment suited for the treasure basket. We then observed using a PCA, recording what happened during the play sessions, with ourselves, as practitioners, observing.

The treasure baskets

As introduced in Xander's play, described in Chapter 2, a treasure basket can include metal, natural mediums, and open ended resources, such as items that on their own could be interpreted as anything the imagine allows, such as a stick. Plastic items are generally avoided. The basket experience allows the baby a satisfying sensory play experience without interference from an adult. However, the presence of the caregiver remains part of the process and the items should be selected with a consideration of their appropriateness to safety and health precautions. Smaller items should be avoided as the need to mouth everything is often met with refusal to allow this sensory experience and therefore reduces the potential of the basket play experience (Goldschmied and Jackson, 2004).

The key areas to note are that:

- Observe the infant rather than intervene;
- There is no right or wrong;
- It should be inclusive and therapeutic; and
- Natural items from everyday life rather than manufactured toys.

As a research practitioner, using a PCA was an approach to help with observations, but we also wanted to ensure that my colleagues and I understood what this meant. We drew on Carl Rogers (1970) and I wanted the approach to enable the infants to consider and acknowledge their own feelings in their play. I wanted to let the infants in the group know that it was alright to feel and encourage to process feelings in a safe and constructive way. By providing a free atmosphere within safe boundaries, the adult allowed them complete freedom to express themselves verbally, physically, or with playthings.

A person-centered approach when observing is to be:

- Non-judgmental;
- Non-directive; and
- Non-interpretative (Rogers, 1970).

Using a PCA during treasure basket play, helped us to see and reflect on the play process. The main results drawn from our project were that the infants vocalized and initiated interactions with us during play. They were initially unsure of how to use equipment and mouthed a few items whist beginning to explore them using other senses. Repetitive play was evident during the weeks, but greater independence grew as the time progressed, and smaller groups formed.

The supervision meeting: plenary play session and findings

Initially, as practitioners, we assumed we knew what the infants would want to do and were reacting too quickly. Taking time to respond, rather than immediately stepping into their play, proved more beneficial and allowed us not to lead the play. By mirroring vocalizations and body movements, it seemed that there was increased confidence in their self-exploratory play. We grew to observe without engaging, allowing the wallowing of play to unfold. Being conscious of our own body language and facial expressions, of where we sat and how much note taking we made, also made us much more engaged in our surroundings and, as a result, the observations we created were more detailed in not only how the infant reacted to situations and engaged in their surroundings but why they had done so.

This led us to think more broadly in our planning for the individual interests and strengths of the infants observed.

The post-supervision session also enabled me to probe the practitioner's knowledge and understanding about the infants they cared for as well as supporting their own professional development. It therefore created a space to ensure that the practitioner had growing knowledge and the skills in learning and development, as well as being supported through the process. By developing the small scale project over a period of a few weeks, the needs and abilities of the infants were identified, as well as thinking about their environment, benefits, and challenges This improves not only play practice in the present but the quality of provision offered as a whole, as well as supporting and contributing to the continued professional development of the practitioners working with the infants in the baby room (Norman, 2015; Goldshmied and Jackson, 2004).

Practice of supervision and reflections

As early years practitioners, we are continually thinking about creating exciting learning potentials for the infants we work with. This type of thinking becomes habitual and automatic in our everyday lives. This 'way of being' and reflecting forms our professional identity. Through questioning our actions to why we think about our practice, both beyond and within, the merging of the two in our work setting enables a *professional artistry* to be developed, as described by Schon (1983 and 1987).

In recognizing emotional learning with reflective practice, thinking about the individual process is enhanced. Subjective feelings are associated with the events and this culminates in reflecting on the way outcomes were experienced and differing possible outcomes (Hawkins and Shohet, 2007).

Reflection is therefore used to:

- Theorize our actions;
- Develop confidence;
- Develop an active agent in the daily routine of care;
- Support an agency of change;
- Increase recognition and knowledge that empowers and improves quality;
- Enable our vulnerability to be discussed and shared with colleagues;
- Challenge and develop our own pedagogical thinking; and
- Advocate for children in activity, evaluating multiple perspectives and development.

Reflective practice/practitioner is an increasingly familiar term when working in a caring profession, especially when it is an expected approach to practice and linked to quality improvement.

Reflection in action

Schon (1987) evaluated professionals in how they could 'reflect in action'. Reflecting in action requires practitioners to think spontaneously and work instinctively by drawing on similar experiences to solve problems or make necessary decisions. Schon suggested that reflection in action was prompted by unforeseen situations in daily routines, both positive and negative. It helps to reframe, or look differently at knowledge in action, leading to greater understanding or maybe change.

- *Knowledge in Action – more conscious of this underlying knowledge*
- *Initiative knowledge TO conscious awareness*
- *Links between theory and practice* (Norman, 2019).

By adopting a Person-Centered Planning approach, supervision meetings can be used in a variety of situations, such as when you are supporting someone to plan for their short- and long-term future within a range of different life situations, for example, in education, socially, or through work.

- Help people to work out what they want in their lives.
- Improve understanding about what support a person needs to pursue their dreams and aspirations.
- Help to shape and clarify contributions made from different services and agencies to ensure they are effective in helping people meet their goals.
- Bring together people who have a part to play in supporting people for joint problem solving.

Sometimes new practitioners worry that they are not good enough. This may lead them to worrying about being critical of their own practice. As a lead practitioner, I try to show them that it is OK to feel apprehensive and reflections help them stand back and evaluate the whole situation, not just their own perspective.

Practice is not always perfect but, by reflecting on practice, it creates an added awareness and thinking about continually improving and recognizing that mistakes and unforeseen events. These are all areas that can be used for future learning and improving practice. Taking the time to reflect is therefore helpful to highlighting both the successes and challenges of our work.

5
A community of practice

Teamworking in the baby room

Learning objective

To consider approaches of leading and working together in the baby room.

To develop and establish ways of working together as teams in supporting infants attending the baby room,

A community of practice: teamworking in the baby room

This chapter examines the way a Person-Centered Approach (PCA) could be helpful when working as part of a team in the baby room. I include examples to illustrate how this could be offered as an approach for practice.

Why use a Person-Centered Approach (PCA)

Within my own personal experiences, as well as including the other practitioner voices of working in the baby room, I have been able to turn to a PCA in developing positive regard and caring. When working with teams and leading groups of practitioners, I have also been inspired by a PCA. I have been able to empathize, with the goal of providing genuine understanding about my work. It has also made me think about how I am perceived and project myself as I work in the baby room. My role as a practitioner and my philosophy is something I have developed in thinking how I want to work with children. For me, I think it's about being foregrounded within humanistic psychology.

Through my everyday practice, I have developed confidence, particularly working with young infants, and this extended to my growing confidence in working with parents as it became another thread of my practice. One of the biggest challenges in my growing confidence, however, was working as part of a team. When I first began working with infants, I had not anticipated the challenges I would face in this regard. I felt I was quite authoritarian and got flustered if a colleague rolled their eyes or ignored me. I remember an infant crying while they were being changed and I was trying to tell the practitioner to stop and slow down. Her reaction was very defensive, and I think she felt I was undermining her professional role. I did not feel I was but I think perhaps I could have articulated my concern for the infant differently. Another example was when a young infant, about 18-months-old, was crying and I was supporting her in talking to her in a calm way and helping her with her shoes. I recall a colleague walked in front of me and picked up the infant, with the shoes and walked away. From what I can remember I think she was the key person of the infant but her approach to me was quite challenging and, as a senior colleague, I felt awkward and frustrated. These were few incidents compared to the joys of working with colleagues, but as many of us recognize that we often remember the things that didn't go so well as opposed to the ones that did.

One of the things I noted in my own reflections was that, although I felt I was quite calm, easy going, and relaxed, as well as being listened to, the perception of myself did not always align with how others perceived me. Practitioners I worked with shared that they viewed me as very confident and quite authoritarian in some of my approaches. I reflected on this with some consideration and thought about refocusing my relationships. I wanted to reflect on the philosophy that underpinned the way I worked, and this created numerous self-reflections as I worked as part of a team as well as leading teams. For me, being a leader is about being committed and actively instilling the vision of a PCA. I feel I want to be open and to continually learn about how to include a PCA. For me, it is about consciously holding the positive beliefs about others I work with and the potential they are capable of. In developing their own practice as well developing an equal and ethical partnership, I also think it is about working with others individually. By meeting and discussing their personal goals, beliefs, and values, it promotes a person-centered culture. For me, therefore, it is important to include the value of our everyday interactions, and how we are perceived, as well as routines and systems—the process is all part of a PCA.

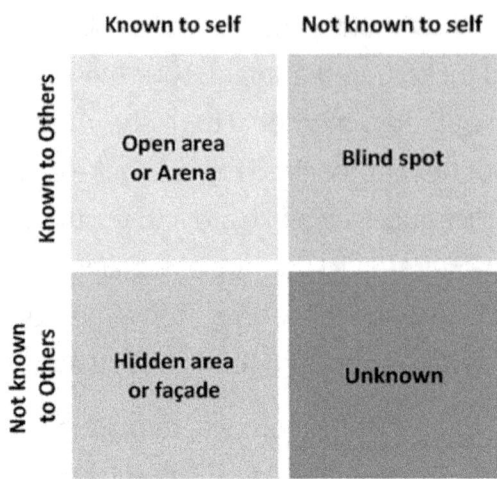

The Johari Window Model

Figure 10 The Johari Window model.

One model that is worth considering when working as a team, is The Johari Window. This model was developed by Luft and Ingham (1955) and is a model that could also be used to enhance the individual's perception about others and themselves. The model, for me, evokes ways about how trusting relationships can be nurtured. By charting the information, the individual areas are revealed to others, as well as learning about themselves from other's feedback. Everyone is represented by the Johari model through four quadrants with each quadrant signifying personal information, feelings, motivation, and whether that information is known or unknown to oneself or others. The Johari window model is therefore used to enhance the individual's perception of others. This model is therefore based on two ideas within trust. This is acquired by revealing information about yourself to others and also learning about yourself from their feedback.

The method of conveying and accepting feedback is interpreted in this model. Two of these quadrants represent self and the other two represent the part unknown to self but to others. The information transfers from one quadrant to the other as the result of shared trust, which can be achieved through socializing and the responses received from others (Luft, 1970).

An example of using The Johari Window model in practice

Cassy recently began placement at a children's center and was going to be attending full time for one year. The team did not know much about her and, in this context, the unknown and hidden areas are larger, and the open area will be small. As the others don't know much about her, the blind spot will also be smaller. During the first couple of weeks, Cassy would spend most of her free time going to the local shops and signing out of the setting, which was her preferred way to spend her breaks. However, her co-workers found her to be quiet, and not very interactive, as well as a little unsociable.

During a meeting and in sharing and talking about the model, Cassy was quite surprised at the way she was perceived and had not thought too much about going out at lunch.

Subsequently, she asked if anyone would like to go with her for a walk and would aim to alternate her time away, sometimes staying and eating lunch with others before going for a walk by herself. She made the effort to be chattier and more open and, very quickly, the team were connecting more and learning about her interests. It wasn't really about her going out at lunch as this was acceptable, but it was more that it had been perceived that she couldn't wait to get away rather than Cassy just wanting a break and some quiet time.

Her hidden and unknown areas became smaller and, although Cassy deliberately chose to keep some of her personal life private, she did reveal other parts of herself and reflected on how she was perceived by others.

As part of a team, I think about how I could re-conceptualize the way I lead and work together. I wanted to resist the hierarchal system often noted in different managerial organizations, including earlier settings, and instead create a distributed type of leadership. This is when everybody takes responsibility and works together for the good of the children and families they serve. For me, it's about being a senior practitioner working in the day-to-day care of the baby room and not being disconnected from those receiving the care offered.

The distinction between managers and leaders is therefore quite important. Leading practice for me is about modelling and critically evaluating my own experiences and with others, consistently aiming for better outcomes with the children they care for. Together, it is about being optimistic about the influence and positive leadership. It is about a shared vision of principles of care. It is also influencing the future and this is very different, in my view, to management. Management is more focused on the planning and organization, coordinating, and controlling systems. For me, I like to think of the team as flourishing and, as a leader, create environments where people can identify and solve problems together as well as individually. By delegating power and responsibility between us as a shared group, members of the team were about the process of working as a team rather than focusing on an end goal. We recognize that, in early years, there can be a high turnover of practitioners in settings for various reasons, from pay to promotion to job dissatisfaction. By empowering and encouraging, the focus is on the process of relationships rather than techniques, following a set of guidelines. It is about establishing a culture of listening, which should have an impact on how staff work together and respect each other.

By considering the process of teams a little further, I have included Tuckman's (1977) group model and, while this could be argued as being quite a dated model, I still feel it is very relevant in the way people come together and work. The process of identifying tensions and then agreeing them as they shape and form as part of a team is central to the model. Tuckman evaluates the development of a group in terms of:

- forming
- storming
- norming
- performing.

This model has been popularized in academic literature and it is significant because it has grown to be important to many different types of groups in workplace environments. I find it helpful in thinking about teams, although I wouldn't take the model literally but rather be informed about the way groups come together and the different things that are happening in that process.'

Stage 1: forming

The first stage is about forming and thinking about orienting to the shared collective rules and meanings of the setting. In this case, the practitioners need to reflect on their interpersonal behaviors with each other as a team. It is also about how the group members establish relationships with the leaders within that group, as well as meeting policy to practice. This forming stage could happen fairly frequently if there is a high turnover of staff, with the dynamics constantly moving and shifting, so this forming is important in terms of thinking about what the shared vision of the baby room is. What are the beliefs and values and the mission statement? What underpins the everyday practice of working with infants?

Stage 2: storming

From this position, the group then move into the storming process. This is a time of potential conflict and into group discussions. It is thinking about, now that we have established all beliefs and values of the room, how do we work within this structure of unity? Of course, in terms of working through this as a process, there is inevitably opposition around relational issues. Groups can move and resist towards the unknown areas of their practice and seek to retain their security. This is particularly relevant when working with infants and thinking about areas such as:

- How do we deal with crying?
- How do we deal with biting?
- How do we deal with the different approaches that perhaps each practitioner performs when working? How do we respond to parents and families?

- When is it in opposition to what we are currently doing in the baby room, for example, insisting that their young child doesn't go to sleep till 3:30 p.m., a time when we would be engaged in play?

Tuckman states that group members can even become quite hostile towards each other and resistant towards a leader, as well, in expressing their individuality and resisting the group's new staff move and entering the team.

An example of this is when I have been a mentor to a new member of staff. I visited her during her first week and completed two meetings to support her settling into a new position. At the end of the second week, an incident arose that I had to deal with. Another more experienced practitioner, who was working closely with her, was worried she looked upset and had started crying to herself when she was supporting the children during an activity. She had been approached several minutes before by the owner. The practitioner asked her if she was alright. She stated yes but appeared upset. I was informed of the incident by a lead practitioner, who felt it needed to be further investigated. I then had a general mentor meeting about how the new staff were getting on in the setting. I spoke to the new practitioner. We looked at how she had settled in generally and drew up a mentoring plan. I discussed areas to develop and areas that were positive.

We focused on three main areas:

1) These were emotional support strategies in relation to supporting infants and their emotional states, and how we perceive crying.

2) I also talked to her about staff collaboration and teamwork, and how this was generally going. She also initiated discussion about her position within the teams and her feelings during the day; feelings of anxiety and of safety.
3) We discussed times that were increasingly stressful for her and other times when she was more relaxed. I also discussed when she felt anxious or upset and calm. She followed this up with the incident about how she needed to understand the observation schedule, alongside meeting regulations.

Stage 3: norming

Moving through the storming stage, there is now a third stage, known as norming. This is where a cohesive group develops. Groups come together and, again, this is why supervision, including groups of supervision, is considered significant. It is about recognizing each other's individuality and the opportunity for them to express their personal opinions. It is about coming together and sharing models and ways of working in harmony. It is also during this stage that the group becomes an entity in and of itself. Everybody knows what their roles and responsibilities are, and this can create a really good feeling around maintaining a shared group identity.

Stage 4: performing

Group conflict during this phase is perceived as actively being avoided to ensure that harmony persists into the next stage, which is known as performing stage. This doesn't mean difficult conversations are not shared or challenges are diminished, but the goal is rather about proactively recognizing these and working through them together constructively. Denying that a problem within the team exists, can reinforce the situation and does not allow the process of movement to shift. Key staff may be viewed as manipulative and therefore destructive in terms of relationship and productivity. This culminates in tension and potentially a future explosive outburst.

When a leader suppresses a problem within the team, both parties could acknowledge that conflict exists but devalue its significance to them. There is an acknowledgement that individuals are not happy but continue suppressing the feelings of those involved. Power positions can also exist in hierarchal teams and may be identified in numerous ways, including experience or possession of higher qualifications. Dominating conversations, interrupting, crying, or non-verbal responses may be illustrated through, for example, demanding changes to a routine. In the long term, this approach will impact relationships and lower the quality-of-care provision (Jones and Pound, 2008, p. 41; Rodd, 2013). "Conflict in early childhood settings is a form of interpersonal interaction where two or more people struggle or compete over claims, beliefs, values, preferences, resources, power, status or any other desire' (Rodd, 2013, p. 105). Recognizing the team issue and addressing it appropriately with respect is the first step.

Performing is therefore about functional role relatedness, as evaluated by Tuckman (1977), as the group adapts and carries out their roles, enhancing task activities and routine of the day structures. This stage is about supporting everybody's roles and responsibilities though flexible functionality. The group's energy is directed to the everyday tasks of caring for each other.

An example of how groups move through the stages is illustrated by the vignette of Lola (the leader) who decided to change the staff's break times, creating two shorter breaks rather than one long break. However, when Lola went on leave for a few days, the team returned to their original way of organizing break times. When Lola returned, she wanted to return to a more fluid approach and, within the team, there was conflict about why they had changed the system back. Lola called a meeting and the practitioners shared their concerns and issues around having shorter breaks. Lola agreed she should have met with each staff member individually and then as a group, working out a solution together to resolve the pressure around lunch time cover. By communicating and meeting, the team worked together to resolve the issue and support each other.

A Person-Centered Approach to resolution

Once the practitioners had met as a team and discussed what had happened, they were able to self-reflect and listen to each other. They discussed the advantages and disadvantages of both ways of working, as well as what the current policies were, the theory, and thinking about the children's voice. They also reflected on their own attitudes and feelings towards children leading their own play and this led to further discussions around freedom with guidance. It also enabled the team to reflect on the meanings around stories beyond language, and they thought about the close, individualized contact between practitioner and infant, the emotional connection, bonding, and attachment opportunities, as well as promoting nurturing independence and creating an enabling environment.

It was agreed to try to be more relaxed in their approaches and responding to the infants needs rather than an 'operational' day aim to create qualitative moments to tune into the infants they care for.

In thinking about the emotional labor of the practitioner's role, this can be apparent as they emotionally invest or choose not to when working with the infants they care for. The baby room care of infants can be emotionally exhausting work and it is often assumed that practitioners have a maternal instinct, which is why they choose the job they do. This not only undermines the profession but is a dis-service in terms of thinking about how practitioners work and what is expected of them emotionally. Many of the practitioners working in the baby room are those with the least experiences and are less qualified than those working with the older children. For practitioners to thrive as a team, these issues need to be highlighted and addressed at national and international level, investing in early years in the long term. What would this investment look like?

Why is Tuckman relevant to the baby room?

In the twenty-first century, there continues to be a call for improved accessibility to qualifications and, rather than creating more flexibility to staffing ratios), more investment into the sector is needed at a national level. Drawing on Tuckman's model, a concern from a personal perspective is that early year's teams are susceptible to being perpetually at the forming and storming stages of group formation.

The Social Mobility Commission in England published a report (2020) and concluded that the 37 per cent of early year's workers left their employer within two years (Gov.UK, 2020).

The commission warned that this high turnover of staff impacts the quality of service offered by early year's providers as well as the children's outcomes. While this was from 2020, the impact of the pandemic is likely to have worsened these trends and caused a rise in figures. Early year's practitioners often have a high workload and many responsibilities. Many workers said that their work included heavy cleaning tasks, including washing windows and cleaning floors, as well as highlighting the low pay rates in the sector. Many childcare workers reported working at second jobs to help make ends meet. Early year's staff were also found to work longer hours than comparable occupations, with findings that full-time early year's staff could work more than 42 hours a week (Lawler, 2020). This was an area I found ethically challenging; thus, rather than going home when I should have, I would often work up to ten hours a day to ensure everyone was supported and nurtured. However, the pace was challenging, and the responsibility was demanding. I did recognize that this is something I should have challenged further with the senior team, but as manager this can be quite difficult. I also think this is where pastoral care, supervision, and access to counselling are vital for staff to be able to work for long hours with young infants. Being able to express and share worries, successes, and challenges in confidence without feeling professionally compromised are all helpful in and providing a high quality service underpinned by a PCA.

Staffing issues and being professional in the baby room is underpinned by many factors when working together as a team with infants. Considerations about valuing the times for teams to grow together, improve retention, and support leaders through continuous professional development, and wages, are all areas that can have a lasting impact on the sector. At a local level, it could also facilitate ways of moving teams from storming to norming, to flourishing and creative teams with a sense of wellbeing. PCA underpins an approach at local level that values the individuals within the team, acknowledging the long-term investment in individuals to thrive.

Person-centered teams

Developing a PCA in teams means that managers and leaders need to involve support staff in the decision-making, discover the existing skills and interests of staff, and see how these can be used to support the infants and families in the baby room to find out their concerns and what support is needed. This goes for the staff team too, so everyone works together, which inevitably changes thinking within power relationships. It is suggested that when formal day care settings operate by encouraging power relationships with staff, they typically mirror that relationship with the children they support, acting as if they oversee and are in charge of them rather than with them. All relationships within organizations need to be based on 'power-with' because 'power-over' culminates in rights being removed and one voice dominating the relationship (McCormack and McCance, 2010).

The value of working-together teams

As with person-centered planning, the process of developing person-centered teams begins with getting to know each other, their skills, interests, and support needs. The families and infants attending the baby room should always takes priority in this process. The team and leader have three important interfaces:

1) With the individuals they support;
2) With the baby room community and wider community of the formal day care settings. Their characteristics reflect the values and skills of the community; and
3) Developing community relationships, supporting each other, and influencing good quality practice.

Leading a team though a PCA involves leaders who are:

- Self-aware but also know how to recognize their emotions.
- Able to emotionally hold their team.
- Effective communicators and clearly express their thoughts.
- Socially aware so they can view and appreciate what is happening and give valuable feedback.
- Able to support conflict resolution, effectively managing conflicts and offering resolution.
- Respectful to others.
- Able to recognize they may need to o change and learn from their own mistakes and failures to develop.
- Able to engage in active listening and celebrating feedback (Sanderson, 2022. np).

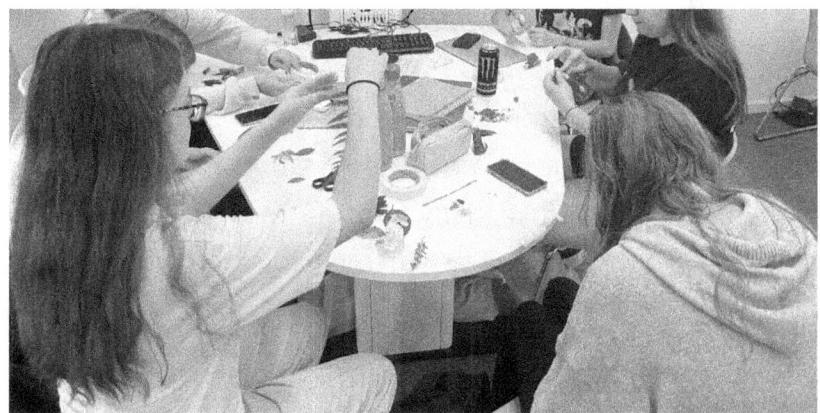

Figure 11 Being creative as part of a team through activities.

One example in thinking about teams further could be to draw a circle on a piece of paper and then think back over the last 24 hours. How many people have you engaged with and how did you feel; were you the sad self, the happy self, or the child self? Draw those parts in the circle. These are the configurations of the self.

Mearns and Thorne (2000) developed this idea, suggesting that each person has multiple configurations of self, made up of 'elements which form a coherent pattern generally reflective of a dimension of existence within the Self' (p. 102). The concept of configurations of the self is that various alternative personalities develop and are projected in certain circumstances. Each configuration has its own desires, needs, style, and view of the world. During a typical day, a practitioner may draw on various configurations of themselves. By exploring, reflecting, and examining configurations of self in a safe, non-threatening, and non-judgmental environment, the practitioner may have an increased awareness and, therefore, the opportunity to process their feelings, thoughts, and behaviors to contextualize the reality and impact of how they were in given situations. This could be a helpful activity for those working with infants and sharing the dialogue about their roles in working with infants.

They may reflect on whether they feel happier at certain times of the day, less confident in others, or anxious at the end of the day. As a leader, it is not about analyzing the configurations of the practitioner's self but sharing the knowledge and supporting the practitioner by offering empathy, understanding, and an authentic interest in how they feel as they choose to explore parts of themselves in their daily practice. In a sense, it is a reminder of developing and articulating how to be emotionally iterate within oneself and moving beyond how a person behaved. By reflecting on how the emotions of the inner moves to the outer, as a process, we are then able to think about others and the children we care for, being able to co-regulate their emotions more authentically and with understanding. It is therefore connected to Rogers' idea of conditional positive regard that a person may increase their own self-acceptance when they gain a sense of worth and understanding about themselves and others. Teamwork is about treating people as individuals, respecting their rights, developing mutual trust and understanding, and developing person-centered relationships.

Summary of team beliefs and values with a PCA

To create a values-based, person-centered outlook, teams express their sense of compassion and values of care. This could be achieved through:

- Creating situations where people identify what really matters to others throughout their daily work;
- Using a variety of communicative activities;
- Developing relationships so autonomy grows, and practitioners can express their concerns and ideas within the team; and
- Distributing leadership roles while trusting and respecting the sharing of information and confidentiality.

It is easy to devalue just how intense team working is within the baby room. Working with infants is complex and emotionally demanding. Working with other adults is a separate set of skills again, as opposed to an extension of the childcare being provided. Many practitioners are not supported or given the space to reflect on working with others and the focus is predominately on the infant they are caring for, while juggling parental requests and the daily routine. Certainly, as a manager for many years in a busy day nursery, I knew my own professionalism was challenged by conflicts, change of team members, and miscommunication. In drawing on a PCA, it aims to offer one approach to be able to consider how a leader is challenged but also reassured of the dynamics of how a group works.

For me, the nuggets of help were essentially:

- Working together is about recognizing individual flaws and assets they can bring to the group;
- Perceptions and realities of individuals can be fluid in a team;
- Listening is valuable;
- Models and theory aid the recognition about how teams are a continual process rather than a fixed entity; and
- Emotional labor in the baby room is central to how teams operate.

Conclusion

Picture portraits to practice: an application of including a PCA

This final chapter brings together some of the key themes from the previous chapters and provides a summary of application to practice that might prove fruitful for practitioners embarking on or currently in practice within the baby room. The intention is therefore to actively engage with this chapter as a way of sharing, discussing, reflecting, and processing a PCA.

The key features of a PCA for practitioners working in the baby room are:

- The individual (person) is at the center;
- Family members and those involved in a child's care are full partners, actively involved;
- Planning for the child reflects their capacities, what is important to them, as well as the support needed to develop and make a valued contribution to their community; and
- There is a shared commitment to action that considers the child's agency of voice and rights.

Working within formal day care where a PCA is encouraged, includes a commitment to team working while simultaneously placing the child at the heart of their thinking. Some key areas that are considered in working within a PCA is:

- Individuals are open to continual learning about how to implement a PCA into their practice;
- The practitioners consciously hold positive beliefs about their children they educate as well as those working with them and beyond, including parents;
- Practitioners focus on the individual's potential not their deficit;
- Practitioners develop equal and ethical partnerships with families of the children in their care;
- Practitioners work and support the child as an individual in meeting their needs;
- A PCA is developed and included within supervision and parent partnerships; and
- A 'person-centered culture' is promoted, whereby behaviors and language, as well as systems and processes, are person-centered.

A Person-Centered Approach (PCA) to a CRIB of Care
Baby room relationships in formal day care

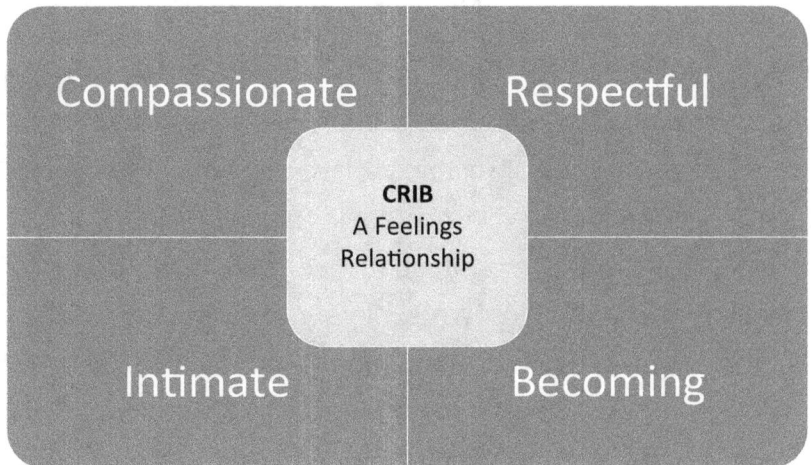

A Person-Centered Approach (PCA) to a CRIB of Care
Baby room relationships in formal day care

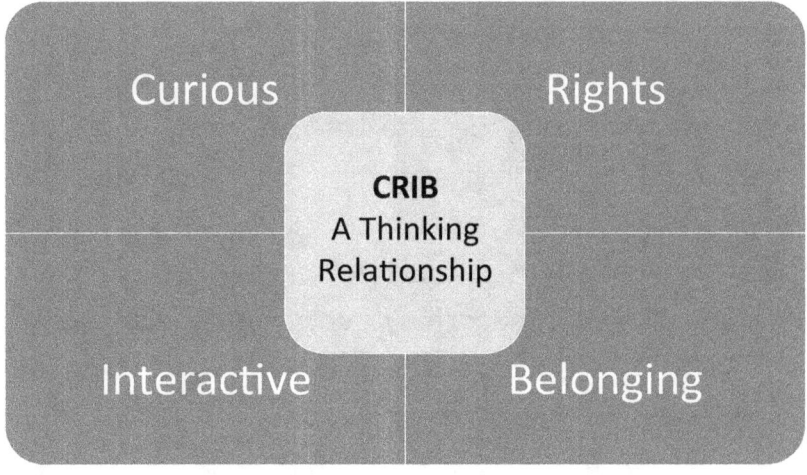

In thinking about the models further, I have outlined some examples of infants I have worked with to illustrate the way a PCA could be applied to everyday practice. I haven't responded to the questions but rather included them as a way of posing discussions and reflective thoughts about practice.

The purpose of each portrait is to reflect on each one and, as a group, team, or individual, consider responses to the questions posed. The portraits, while fictitious, have all been written as typical scenarios I have faced in working in the baby room. They are therefore representative of situations and events and the questions are prompts to drill down, explore, and examine how a PCA could be used in each portrait. Information may be gathered using the previous chapters to consider possible solutions. Each portrait also invites the reader to continue developing further examples relevant to their own experiences and contexts that could be shared and resolved using a PCA.

Picture portrait 1
Context

Pandora began nursery at seven months of age. She has two parents who both work, with one returning from maternity leave. Pandora started nursery because her parents were returning to work and there was little alternative. Pandora had previously attended singing clubs and sensory clubs with her mother. However, she had not been separated from her mother and only met others with her. Pandora has recently been offered milk in a bottle, with the introduction of food, as well as continuing with being breastfed in the evening.

Focused questions

How could the practitioners support Pandora through a PCA? Below are some considerations with reference to the PCA model.
Can you reflect any more from experience and practice?

Picture portrait 2
Context

Ash is a new member of staff, who recently qualified as a practitioner and can support and lead a small group of children. He is quite anxious about starting somewhere new and has only had experience of placement practice. Below are some considerations with reference to the PCA model.

Focused questions

How could the practitioners support Ash through a PCA?
Consider the PCA model and how this may be helpful in ways to support Ash.
Can you reflect any more from experience and practice?

Picture portrait 3
Context

Sam is nine months of age and has just settled into the baby room. He has a small cuddly blanket and likes to have it with him at all times. The team are unsure if they should be encouraging Sam to put the cuddly away or not worry about him having it. He seems more settled with the cuddly nearby. This has prompted questions about personal items, such as blankets and teddies, in the baby room. One practitioner has done some research on transitional objects and has planned a talk about attachment.

Focused questions

What would you do in this situation?
If you were considering a PCA, would encouraging or discouraging the cuddly be because you or Sam were unsure about what to do?
How would the talk guide the practice and how would this be helpful?

Picture portrait 4
Context

Sue is a parent and, with her partner Gill, they have decided to bring their child to the baby room. They are keen for their child to remain gender neutral and have had many discussions with the manager. The staff are unsure if this means with toys, equipment, or more generally, such as language.

Focused questions

How could the practitioners be supported by the parents and take the lead from them?
What discussions could be had with the manager?
What is a PCA here?

Picture portrait 5
Context

Carla is 11-months-old and has been settling in for a few weeks. However, she is still feeling very unsettled during her time in the baby room and crying a lot. Her parents are beginning to wonder if this is the right place for her and the tensons are building in the partnership between the parents and the practitioners.

Focused questions

How could you support Carla and why are the settling in sessions not working for her?
What could you do in the baby room?
How could you support the parents in their decisions?
How could you be person-centered in your approach?

Practitioners who attend to the individual needs of each infant, enables them the ability to be and feel heard, encouraging a holistic approach to learning that supports their personal, social, and emotional development. By referring to the model, a PCA is viewed as an approach that is underpinned by theoretical thinking but also meaningful to practice in many ways. By providing a few examples, it is hoped that the PCA will be a source of information and inspiration to those working with infants in the baby room and they are perhaps familiar examples. Caring for the emotional wellbeing of infants has always been at the heart of practice and, in contemporary practice, this continues to be essential for all early year's community members, through to parents and practitioners. Adopting a PCA provides an opportunity to reflect, feel nurtured, and thrive together, with a sense of belonging.

Recommended discussion topics

Leading practice
- What factors are necessary for effective leadership?
- How could you lead a successful team in the baby room?
- Why is leadership important in the baby room?

Working with parents
- If you are caring for infants in the baby room, why is the relationship with their parents essential?
- What methods could be effective in working with parents?

Supervision
- Why is creating one-on-one, as well as group time with staff, important?
- What distinguishes supervision from appraisals?
- How could you develop and facilitate group supervision?

Working with infants
- What is your understanding of ethical care?
- How is working with infants emotionally challenging?
- What is the importance of attachment led care through a Person-Centered Approach (PCA)?
- How do you work inclusively in the baby room?

Discussion topics
To consider
The baby room is a complex and challenging place to work with domestic duties being extremely important alongside caring for the infants. Drawing on Goouch and Powell (2010), *The Baby Room* project (OUP) considers how singing and lullabies in the baby room can enhance emotional wellbeing as well as create effective relationships.

Case study
Jack started in the baby room and is seven months of age. He seems to have settled in well and has been attending for a week so far. However, the last few days he seems to be increasingly agitated when he is dropped off at the beginning of the day and picked up at the end of the day by his parents. During the day he seems to be enjoying himself, although he is observed to be quite anxious at mealtimes and when the routine is changed.

Consider what could be happening
Reflect on transitional times and theories of attachment, and discuss the key person's role and why this is distinct from the general role of earliest practitioner.

Reflect on the emotional labor of the key person and how they could be supported in the care of Jack through a PCA.

By answering the above, create a plan highlighting the key areas of care. Working through a PCA ensures:

- Empathy
- Congruence
- Unconditional positive regard.

Ensure all three are included in the plan.

References

Axline, V. M. (1974). *Play therapy*. New York, NY: Ballantine Books.

Belsky, J., Burchinal, M., McCartney, K., Vandell, D., Clarke-Stewart, K. and Owen, M. (2007). Are There Long Term Effects of Early Child Care? *Child Development*, 78(2), pp. 681–701.

Berne, E. (1958). Transactional analysis: A new and effective method of group therapy. American Journal of Psychotherapy, 12(4), pp. 735–743.

Blaiklock, K. (2013) Talking with Children When Using Prams While Shopping. NZ Research in *Early Childhood Education Journal*. 16(15 – 28). at: https://www.childforum.com/images/stories/2013_Blaiklock_published.pdf. [Accessed 19 June 2023].

Bowlby, J. (1969). Attachment. Attachment and loss: Vol. 1. Loss. New York, NY: Basic Books.

Bowlby, J. (1953). Childcare and the growth of love. Harmondsworth, UK: Penguin.

Bowlby, J. (1988). *A Secure Base: Clinical Applications of Attachment Theory*. London, UK: Routledge.

Bowlby, J. (2005). *The Making and Breaking of Affectionate Bonds*. London, UK: Routledge.

Brazelton, T. (1990) *The earliest relationship*. USA: Perueus Books.

Bronfenbrenner, U. (1979). *The ecology of human development: Experiments by nature and design*. Cambridge, MA: Harvard University Press.

Brooker, L. (2010). Constructing the triangle of care: power and professionalism in staff/parent relationships. *British Journal of Educational Studies*, 58(2), pp. 181–196.

Brookfield, S. (1995). *Becoming a Critically Reflective Teacher*. San Francisco, CA: Jossey-Bass.

Carroll, D. W. (2013). Stress, coping, and growth. In D. W. Carroll, Families of children with developmental disablities: Understanding stress and opportunities for growth (pp. 31–44). American Psychological Association. https://doi.org/10.1037/14192-003

Corey, G. (1996). *Theory Practice of Counselling and Psychotherapy*. Second Edition. Pacific Grove, CA: Brooks/Cole Publishing Company, pp. 89–129, 196–219.

Cousins, S. (2017). Practitioners' constructions of love in early childhood education and care, *International Journal of Early Years Education*, 25(1), pp. 16–29, DOI: 10.1080/09669760.2016.1263939

Dunn, Judith F., eds. (1994). Stepfamilies: who benefits? who does not? Hillsdale, N.J.: L. Erlbaum. Health_Child_Programme. pdf *Education Research Journal*, 14(2), pp. 81–98.

Elfer, P. (2007). 'Infants and young children in nurseries: using psychoanalytic ideas to explore tasks and interactions' *Children and Society*, 21, pp. 111–122.

Gerber, M. (2003). *Dear Parent: Caring for Infants with Respect*. UK. Resources for Infant Edu carers. Revised ed. Edition UK.

Gerber, M. (2001). *Respecting Infants: A New Look at Magda Gerber's RIE Approach. Zero to three*. UK. National Centre for Infants. McGrawHill. ISBN 978-0-9637902-3-1.

Goldschmied, E. and Jackson, S. (2004). *People under three. Young children in day care*. London: Routledge.

Goouch, K. and Powell, S. (2010) *The Baby Room Project*. UK: Esmée Fairbairn Foundation.

Gov.UK (2020). The Social Mobility Commission. [Online] Available at https://www.gov.uk/government/news/stability-of-the-early-years-workforce-in-england-report

Hanson, K. (2012) cited in L. Trodd, (ed) (2015) *The Early Years Handbook for Students and Practitioners*. London, UK: Routledge.

Hawkins, P. and Shohet, R. (2007). *Supervision in the helping professions* (3rded.). Milton Keynes, UK: Open University Press.

Heidegger, M (1990). *Being and Time* Paperback London. Blackwell.

Hess, A. (1980). Training models and the nature of psychotherapy supervision. In A. Hess (Ed.), *Psychotherapy supervision: Theory, research and practice*. New York, NY: John Wiley, Pp.15–25.

Hoffman, I. Z. (1994). Dialectical thinking and therapeutic action in the psychoanalytic process. *The Psychoanalytic Quarterly*, 63(2), 187–218.

Horvath, J. (20221) *Louder than Words* in https://medium.com/the-creative-mind/carl-rogers-on-therapy-reconciling-internal-conflict-1c80bb811979 [Accessed 28 Aug 2021]. *https://ndna.org.uk/face-to-face-training/nursery-training-induction-supervision-and-appraisal/*

Jones, C., and Pound, L. (2008). *Leadership And Management In The Early Years: From Principles To Practice*. McGraw Hill and Education. Maidenhead, UK: OUP.

Lave, J. and Wenger, E. (1991). *Situated learning: Legitimate peripheral participation*. Cambridge, UK: Cambridge University Press.

Lawler, R. (2020). Childcare workers. [Online] Early years alliance. Available at: https://www.eyalliance.org.uk/news/2020/08/report-says-childcare-workers-are-%E2%80%9Cunderpaid-overworked-and-undervalued%E2%80%9D [Accessed 14 Dec 2022].

Louis, S. (2020). How to Use Work Group Supervision to Improve Early Years Practice London, UK: Routledge.

Luft, J. (1970). Group processes; an introduction to group dynamics (second edition). Palo Alto, CA: National Press Books.

Luft, J. and Ingham, H. (1955). *'The Johari window, a graphic model of interpersonal awareness', Proceedings of the western training laboratory in group development.* Los Angeles, CA: UCLA.

Maslow, A. (1962). *Toward a Psychology of Being.* US: Martino Publishing.

McCormack, B. and McCance, T. (2016). *Person-Centred Practice in Nursing and Health Care: Theory and Practice,* 2nd Edition. London, UK: Wiley-Blackwell.

Mearns, D. and Thorne, B. (2000). *Person-Centred Therapy Today: New Frontiers in Theory and Practice.* London, UK: Sage.

Moon, H (2013) *Cherish the First six weeks.* UK. Three Rivers Press.

Norman, A. (2019). *From Conception to Two Years: Development Policy and Practice.* London, UK: Routledge.

Norman, A., & Byrne, J. (2019). Symbolic gesturing: creating opportunities for emotional connections between practitioners and infants in day care. Early Child Development and Care, 191(10), 1577–1589. https://doi.org/10.1080/03004430.2019.1659787

Norman, A. (2022b). A Mentoring Project (part 2). Early Years Educator, [online] 23(8), pp. 23–24. Available at: https://www.magonlinelibrary.com/doi/abs/10.12968/eyed.2022.23.8.23 [Accessed 14 May 2022].

Norman, A. (2022a). A Mentoring Project. Early Years Educator, [online] 23(7), pp. 25–27. Available at: https://www.magonlinelibrary.com/doi/abs/10.12968/eyed.2022.23.7.25 [Accessed 15 May 2022].

Norman, A. (2015). Observing discovery play. Early Years Educator 2015, [online] 16(9), pp. 27–30. Available at: https://www.magonlinelibrary.com/doi/pdfplus/10.12968/eyed.2015.16.9.27?-casa_token=mWTzh5fvkvwAAAAA:zueTwkTxPM75wBTJo1YiITFsWN6UfYbTIwFm9z_LgFexPdV-hvOHoytX8dSXSkUeRc7OBgUfrS0

Nutbrown, C. and Page, J. (2013). *Working with babies and children*. London, UK: Sage.

Page, J. (2017). Reframing infant-toddler pedagogy through a lens of professional love: Exploring narratives of professional practice in early childhood settings in England. *Contemporary Issues in Early Childhood,* [online] 18(4), pp.387–399. Available at: http://journals.sagepub.com/doi/abs/10.1177/1463949117742780

PTUK. (2022) at www.ptuk.com

Rodd, J. (2013). *Leadership In Early Childhood* (3rd edition). Maidenhead, UK: Open University Press (OUP).

Rogers, C. (1969). *Freedom to Learn: A View of What Education Might Become.* Columbus, OH: Charles E. Merrill Publishing Company.

Rogers, C. (1951). *Client-Centered Therapy*. NY: Constable.

Rogers, C. (1961). *On Becoming a Person: A Therapist's View of Psychotherapy.* Boston MA: Houghton Mifflin.

Rogers, C. (1970). *Carl Rogers on Encounter Groups.* New York, NY: Harper and Row.

Rogers, C. (1980) in H. C. Lyon, Jr., and C. R. Rogers. (1981). *On Becoming a teacher.* Columbus, OH: Merill.

Rogers, C. R. (1980). *A Way of Being.* Boston, MA: Houghton Mifflin.

Rogers, C. R. (1951). Client-Centered Therapy: Its Current Practice, Implications, and Theory. Boston, MA: Houghton Mifflin.

Rutter, M. (2002). Nature, Nurture and Development: From Evangelism, through Science towards Policy and Practice. *Child Development*, 73(1), pp. 1–21.

Sanders, P. (2021). *First Steps in Counselling (5th Edition): An Introductory Companion.* London, UK: PCCS Books.

Sanderson, H. (2022). Person centred teams in Person-Centred Teams : [online] Available at: https://pathwaysassociates.co.uk/Archive/pcp/docs/pcteams2.pdf [Accessed 25 Apr 2020].

Schaffer, H. and Emerson, P. (1964). The development of social attachments in infancy. Monographs. Society for Research in Child Development, pp. 1–77.

Schön, D. (1983). *The Reflective Practitioner*. USA: Basic Books.

Schön, D. (1987). *Educating the Reflective Practitioner*. San Francisco, CA: Jossey Bass.

Taggart, G. (2016). Compassionate pedagogy: the ethics of care in early childhood professionalism. *European Early Childhood Education Research Journal*, 24(2), pp. 173–185. DOI: 10.1080/1350293X.2014.970847

Tolan, J. (2003). *Skills in Person-Centred Counselling & Psychotherapy*. London. Sage Publications Ltd

Trevarthen, C. (2001) Intrinsic motives for companionship in understanding; their origin development and their significance for mental health. *Infant Mental Health Journal*. 22.95–131.

Trevarthen, C. (1993) Predispositions to cultural learning in young infants. *Behavioral and Brain Sciences*. 16(3), 534–535.

Tronick, E., Messinger, D., Weinberg, M., Lester, M., LaGasse, L., Seifer, R. and Liu, J. (2005). Cocaine Exposure Is Associated with Subtle Compromises of Infants' and Mothers' Social-Emotional Behavior and Dyadic Features of Their Interaction in the Face-to-Face Still-Face Paradigm. *Developmental Psychology*, [online] 41(5), pp. 711–722. http://dx.doi.org/10.1037/0012-1649.41.5.711

Tuckman, B. W. and Jensen, M. A. (1977). Stages of small-group development revisited. *Group and Organization Studies*, 2(4), pp. 419–427.

Vorria (2003) in C. Nutbrown, and J. Page, eds. (2008). *Working with babies and children from birth to three.* London, UK: Sage.

Ward et al. (2012) in L. Trodd, ed. (2016). *The Early Years Handbook for Students and Practitioners An essential guide for the foundation degree and levels 4 and 5.* London, UK: Routledge. Available at: www.gov.uk/government/uploads/system/uploads/attachment_data/file/180919/DFE-00177-2011.pdf [Accessed 15 Nov 2021]

Zeedyk, S. (2008) Infant buggies may undermine child development. *Observational study.* University of Dundee. UK.

Recommended further readings

Arnott, L. and Wall, K. (2022). *The Theory and Practice of Voice in Early Childhood: An International Exploration.* London, UK: Routledge.

Axline, V. (2022). Dibbs. London, UK: Penguin.

Geldard, K. (2001). *Working with Children in Groups: A Handbook for Counsellors, Educators and Community Workers.* London, UK: Palgrave.

Grimmer, T. (2021). *Developing a Loving Pedagogy in the Early Years: How Love Fits with Professional Practice.* London, UK: Routledge.

hooks, b. (2008) *Belonging.* London. Routledge.

Lave, J. and Wenger, E. (1991). *Situated learning: Legitimate peripheral participation.* Cambridge, UK: Cambridge University Press.

Sanders, P. (2012). The Tribes of the Person-centred Nation: an Introduction to the Schools of Therapy Related to the Person-centred Approach. London, UK: PCCS Books.

Index

appraisals. 3, 87, 92

attachment theory. 63, 69

attuned. 23, 78, 94

autobiographical (personal) lens. 7, 9

Axline, V.M.. 21

baby signing. 68

belonging; PCA. 1; sense of. 16, 26, 30, 37, 64, 137; teamworking. 29

Bowlby, J.. 32, 69, 72

Bronfenbrenner, U. 65

Brookfield, S.. 5, 6

community of infants. *See also* infants; case studies; exploration. 36; feeding. 41, 43; introduction to infant. 38, 39, 44, 45, 49, 50, 54, 57, 61; nappy changing. 40; reflections of practice. 46, 47, 51, 52, 55, 56, 58, 60, 62, 63; sense of belonging. 37; formal day care, in England. 35

community of practice; and practitioners. 31; baby room. 85; building communities. 7; PCA. 1, 14, 30, 85, 102; teamworking in baby room. 111; through observations. 102

community, baby room. 60, 61, 65

congruent. 27, 32

connections; between home and family. 56; caring. 43; emotional. 122; to individual children. 93; to infant. 66

co-practitioners (colleagues) lens. 7

development; and everyday experiences. 57; and learning. 94; and reflection. 88; and wellbeing. 82; child. 93, 101, 102; emotional. 137; individual growth. 32; infant. 5, 59, 68, 93; language. 72; nurturing. 69; of group. 117; personal. 137; physical. 2; practitioner's. 85; professional. 3, 18, 87, 92, 93, 97, 106, 125; self. 22, 88; self-regulation. 78; social. 137; speech. 50

early education. 7, 11, 58, 81, 101

emotional labour. 8, 92, 123, 130

empathy. 11, 19, 24, 27, 29, 40, 74, 75, 102, 128

ethological theory. 69

experiences; baby room. 63; caring. 3; everyday. 58, 81; infants. 4, 69; interactive. 81; learning. 8; lived. 16, 64; parents'. 18; peak. 26; personal. 1, 9, 36, 37, 112; practitioner's. 20, 22; sensory. 58, 62, 81, 104; shared. 2, 9; supervisees. 102

facilitator. 21

formal day care; baby room relationships. 23, 24, 80, 133; counselling approaches. 20, 21, 22; infants in. 1; power relationships. 125; working in England. 35; working together. 28, 30, 32

fully functioning person. 27

group; care setting. 46; caring. 71; communication. 101; parenting. 19; peers. 49; practitioners. 112; supervision. 86, 93, 95, 100; toddler. 49

group model, Tuckman's; forming. 118; norming. 120; performing. 121, 122; storming. 118, 119

growth; personal. 22, 25, 27, 81; self. 31

home. 26, 30, 58, 60, 62, 65, 71; affection. 48; and family connections. 56; feeding. 11, 41; quality time. 47

homelessness. 19

inclusive. 91, 104

individuals; caring. 2; continual learning. 132; growth and development. 32; infants. 6; needs. 20; relational. 100; relationships. 86

infant (student) lens. 5, 6

infants; and caregiver. 65, 66, 67, 69; caring. 2, 3, 5, 8, 16, 18, 25, 26, 28, 31, 86, 88, 89, 92, 94, 100, 123, 137; communication. 82; community of. *See* community of infants; development, theory, and practice. 5; edu-care approach. 82; emotional regulation. 78; experiences. 75; feeding. 11; in formal day care. 1; mental health. 72; nonverbal. 32; practitioners relationship. 9, 20, 22, 23, 95; professionals working with. 2; sleep. 5; stress levels. 72

internal working models (IWMs). 70

intersubjectivity. 65

Johari window model. 114, 115, 117

key person. viii, 42, 75, 113, 140

leadership; baby room. 31; managerial organisations. 116

roles. 129

listening. 1, 7, 10, 14, 22, 42, 49, 78, 82, 85, 95; active. 102, 126; ethical. 74; in person centred supervision. 96; nonverbal communication. 25; practitioners. 7, 48; without judgment. 19

maternal parenting. 71

mental health. 57, 69, 72

mind mindedness, concept of. 70

nursery nurse qualification. 14

parents; community. 60; experiences. 18; feedback to. 8; home feeding. 11; interactions. 50; maternal parenting. 71; partnership. 91; recordings for. 30; relationships. 8; sharing. 83; them and us approach. 18

pedagogy. 82

peers. vii, 47, 49, 53, 56, 87

person centred thinking. 86

Person-Centred Approach (PCA); and thinking. 14; benefits of using. 112, 113, 115; CRIB of Care. 23, 24, 80; developing and practicing. 14, 15, 18, 20; ethics of care. 74; for practitioners, features. 131; guidance. 126; history of. 25, 27, 28; implementation. 132; integrating counselling approaches. 20, 22; person-centred educational space. 77, 79; picture portraits. 134, 135, 136, 137; purpose of reflection. 3; reflective accounts. 43, 48, 49, 53, 54, 57, 60, 63; sense of belonging. 30; supervision with team members. 85, 95, 98, 111, 133; team beliefs and values. 129; therapeutic relationships. 2; understanding. 14, 33

person-centred teams. *See also* teamwork; beliefs and values. 129; decision-making. 125; leaders. 127, 128; value of working-together teams. 126

play. 35; activities. 43, 46, 52, 54; activity. 4, 6; and communication. 36, 40; experiences. 43, 58; physical. 61; sensory. 104; specialist. vii; therapeutic. 20, 21, 35; therapy. 20; to learning. 10

Professional Love. 75

proto conversations. 66

Rogers, Carl. 1, 9, 10, 27, 31, 77, 81, 83, 100, 102, 104, 128

separation theory. 63

still face experiment. 66

supervision. 50, 90, 91; and appraisals. 87, 89, 92, 93; and reflection. 107, 108; approaching. 95; as listening. 85; collaboration. 96; defined. 88; group. 93, 95; listening. 96; meeting. 108; PCA. 85; person centred. 86; post play session. 105, 106; purpose of. 101; session. 97; supporting supervisors. 99, 100, 102; treasure basket. 104

team; and leader. 126; beliefs. 129; meeting. 76; members. 85; of practitioners. 18; staff. 125; working together with. 28, 112, 113, 114, 122

teamwork; beliefs and values. 129; belonging. 29; community of practice. 111; in baby room. 111; Johari Window model. 114, 115, 117, 119, 120; leaders. 127, 128; Person-Centred Approach. 112, 113, 115; person-centred teams. 125; Tuckman's model. 124, 125; value of. 126

theoretical lens. 9, 10

theory of mind. 71

therapeutic. v, vii, 2, 11, 20, 35, 104

treasure baskets. 58, 103, 105

Tuckman, B. W.. 117, 119, 121, 123

tuning in. 75

unconditional positive regard. 21, 27, 29, 30, 32, 57, 78

understanding. 14, 27; about parents' experiences. 18; empathic. 29, 30, 32; of feelings. 26; of others. 28; theoretical. 22

voice. 25, 32, 78, 96, 122, 125, 131

wellbeing. 21, 82, 92, 95, 125, 137

Wenger, E.. 7

working-together teams. 126, *See also* teamwork

Zeedyk, S.. 71

www.ingramcontent.com/pod-product-compliance
Lightning Source LLC
Chambersburg PA
CBHW070808230426
43665CB00017B/2529